# BOOKS I. AND II. OF THE AN... ꭼUSTUS
# HENRY BEESLY AND CORNELIUS TACITUS

**Publisher's Note**

The book descriptions we ask booksellers to display prominently warn that this is an historic book with numerous typos or missing text; it is not indexed or illustrated.

The book was created using optical character recognition software. The software is 99 percent accurate if the book is in good condition. However, we do understand that even one percent can be an annoying number of typos! And sometimes all or part of a page may be missing from the book. Or the paper may be so discolored from age that it is difficult to read. We apologize and gratefully acknowledge Google's assistance.

After we re-typeset and design a book, the page numbers change so the old index and table of contents no longer work. Therefore, we usually remove them.

Our books sell so few copies that you would have to pay hundreds of dollars to cover the cost of proof reading and fixing the typos, missing text and index. Therefore, whenever possible, we let our customers download a free copy of the original typo-free scanned book. Simply enter the barcode number from the back cover of the paperback in the Free Book form at www.general-books.net. You may also qualify for a free trial membership in our book club to download up to four books for free. Simply enter the barcode number from the back cover onto the membership form on the same page. The book club entitles you to select from more than a million books at no additional charge. Simply enter the title or subject onto the search form to find the books.

If you have any questions, could you please be so kind as to consult our Frequently Asked Questions page at www.general-books.net/faqs.cfm? You are also welcome to contact us there. General Books LLC™, Memphis, USA, 2012.

⁃⁃ ⁃⁃ ⁃⁃ ⁃⁃ ⁃⁃ ⁃⁃ ⁃⁃ ⁃⁃

Augustan age, till surging sycophancy scared them away. As for Tiberius, Gaius, Claudius, and

Nero, while they were at the head of affairs themselves, history was falsified from terror, and after their death was narratedf under the influence of still rankling detestation. Induced by this, I purpose to write a short summary of the career J of

Augustus, with its close; and then to recount the reign of Tiberius and his successors without passion and without prejudice, since I am out of the reach of any such temptations.

R.c. 42. 2. When, after Brutus and Cassius were killed, *Cmtraiis*there was no force left in arms for the Common-'*oflugS!*

R.c. 36. wealth; when Pompeius § had been crushed in ,

Sicily; when, now that Lepidus was shelved and

Antonius slain, not even the Julian party had any leader left but Caesar, *he,* divesting himself of his title of Triumvir, proclaimed himself Consul, and,

for the protection of the Commons, satisfied with the privileges of Tribune. Winning over the soldiers by bounty, the populace by grants of corn,

the nation at large by the proffered sweets of repose, step by step he kept mounting higher and higher, centering in his own person the legislative and executive functions, with no man to withstand him. For the boldest had fallen in battle

'Florens,' as used in Tacitus, can seldom be translated exactly, without resorting to a colloquialism. Here it means more than 'during the life of.' 'To the fore ' is what is meant.

t 'Compositse ' may mean ' distorted.

' % 'Summary of the career.' Or the words may mean 'briefly to summarise the close of Augustus's career.' But Tacitus has, as a matter of fact, done more than this.

§ 'Pompeius.' Sextus Pompeius, conquered by Agrippa.

'Tribune.' As such his person was inviolable and he could veto any legislative measure. or proscription, and as for the surviving nobles,

the closer a man hugged his chains the faster he was promoted to rank and riches. Moreover,

enriched by the new *regime,* they preferred the security of the present to the risks of the past.

Nor were the provinces averse to this settlement,

distrusting the government of the Senate and

People on account of the squabbles of partyleaders, the greed of officials, and the impotence to give them redress of laws which intimidation,

intrigue, and, above all, corruption trampled under foot.

3. Moreover, as buttresses to his power, Au-*Augustus's*

gustus elevated Claudius Marcellus, his sister's son, *consolidate*

while still extremely young, to the Pontificate and *an/make*

Curule iEdileship; and Marcus Agrippa, a man '

of low extraction but of distinguished military talents and the partner of his triumphs, to two successive consulships, subsequently selecting him

R.c. 23. as his son-in-law on Marcellus's death. His stepsons, Tiberius Nero and Claudius Drusus, he dignified with the imperial title even before he had suffered any bereavement in his own family. For he had adopted Agrippa's sons Gaius and Lucius as Cassars, and when they had not yet put off the garb of boyhood it was the fondest wish of his heart, in spite of his affectation of refusal, that they should be styled Leaders of the Juniors, and

R.c. 12. declared Consuls. After Agrippa's decease Lucius A.d. 2.

A.d. 4. Caesar on his march to the

armies of Spain, Gaius while returning from Armenia and suffering from a wound, were cut off, either by a natural premature death, or by their grandmother Livia's B.c. 9. treachery; and as Drusus had long previously died, Nero was left the sole surviving stepson, and the centre to which the whole system gravitated. He was adopted as son, co-emperor, colleague in the Tribunician power, and paraded through the armies not as hitherto through his mother's underhand intrigues, but at her open instigation. For she had brought Augustus in his old age so completely under her influence that he drove Pianosa. away to the island of Planasia his sole surviving grandson Agrippa Postumus, who, though devoid, it is true, of accomplishments, and with a boorish pride in his brute strength, was convicted however of no positive crime. Still, to be sure, he made Germanicus—Drusus's son—commander of eight legions on the Ehine, and ordered Tiberius to adopt him, though Tiberius himself had a young son. But no doubt his object was to fence himself with as many safeguards as he could. At that time no war remained on hand except that against the Germans, which was more to wipe away the stain

A. D. 9. of the loss of Quintilius Varus and his army, than from any wish to extend the empire or for any adequate inducement. At home there was peace. Official titles at least remained unaltered. The younger generation had been born since the victory

B. C. 3i. of Actium, and the majority even of old men during the civil wars. Few, indeed, were the men who had seen the Commonwealth.

4. Thus it was that in this revolutionised con-*position of* stitution, the old-fashioned, sound morality had *H'* quite died out. Throwing away the equality of-TM the citizen, all men hung upon the lips of a Prince.

There was no immediate cause for apprehension while Augustus in unimpaired vigour maintained his personal though 'Leaders of the Juniors.' They walked at the head of the sons of senators and patricians at public ceremonies. and domestic prosperity and the public peace. But as old age crept on, and he became besides worn out by disease, and as his approaching end promised the advent of a new era, here and there a man would idly descant on the blessings of freedom, while the majority trembled at the thought of a war for which others again craved. Most people by far, were engaged in pulling to pieces the reputation of the masters who were soon to rule them by every sort of scandal: 'Agrippa was a savage, and exasperated by disgrace, and too young and inexperienced to be equal to such vast responsibility. Tiberius Nero was of mature age and approved generalship, but steeped in the inveterate and inherent arrogance of the Claudian House, showing, too, many indications of a cruel temper which, though stifled, would break out. Even from his infancy he had been brought up in the reigning family. While a mere youth he was loaded with consulships and triumphs. Even during the years which B.c. 6— he spent in exile at Ehodes under the pretext of retirement he had been only brooding over revenge and hypocrisy and covert lust. There was the mother too with her woman's caprice. They must humour the whims of a woman and a couple of striplings into the bargain, who, for the time, would prove an incubus on the state and would one day tear it piecemeal.' 5. While these and similar topics were being *nines and* canvassed Augustus's state of health became worse, *Xs* and there were people who imputed it to the *!!J?fTM of Tiberius.* guilty practices of his wife. In fact, it had been bruited about that a few months previously ' Augustus, having chosen his confidants, and accompanied only by Fabius Maximus, had crossed over to Planasia to visit Agrippa, and that they had there interchanged many tears and marks of affection; which made men cherish hopes that the young man would eventually be re-established in his grandfather's household.' Maximus had divulged this to his wife Marcia, and she to Livia. Cassar was told of it, and when soon afterwards

Maximus died (whether by his own hand or not was uncertain), Marcia was heard at the funeral bemoaning and cursing herself as the cause of her husband's death. Whatever the real facts were,

hardly had Tiberius entered IUyricum when he received a pressing message from his mother to return, and it is not certain whether he found

Augustus at Nola still breathing or already dead.

For Livia had surrounded the house and all its avenues with vigilant sentries, and favourable bulletins were issued from time to time until, when she had taken such precautions as the crisis suggested, she announced in one and the same breath the death of Augustus and the accession of Nero to the throne.

6. The first atrocity of the new reign was the *Murder of* A.d. u. murder of Postumus Agrippa, whom a centurion, though a resolute man, and though he took him by surprise and unarmed, had hard work to kill. Not one word of explanation did Tiberius vouchsafe to the Senate. His excuse was his father's orders, 'His own hand,' etc. Possibly the words might mean, 'and it was suspected that he met with foul play.' which charged the tribune acting as jailer not to delay Agrippa's execution as soon as he should himself have breathed his last. Often and bitterly, no doubt, had Augustus complained of the young man's disposition, and had procured the Senate's express warrant for his banishment. Still he never steeled himself to inflict death on one of his own family, and it is incredible that he would have put his grandson to death in order to render his stepson more secure. What is more probable is that Tiberius and Livia—he from apprehension, she from the proverbial rancour of a stepmother— hurried on the death of a youth whom they detested and loathed. On the centurion's announcing, in soldier-fashion, the execution of his orders, Tiberius replied that they were no orders of his, and that the centurion must be answerable to the Senate for his act. When this came to the ears of Sallustius Crispus, his confidant, and the man who sent the tribune the warrant, he, fearing lest the

blame of the affair should be thrown on him, as it was equally hazardous to invent a falsehood and to confess the truth, urged on Livia the impolicy of betraying family secrets, friendly advice, and military performance of orders, and of Tiberius sapping the Imperial authority by submitting all subjects to the Senate; for only by accepting undivided responsibility could the Imperial authority be maintained.

7. And now all Rome—consuls, senators, knights *The three* —plunged headlong into slavery. The higher a *ear-ai*man's rank, with the more profound hypocrisy, *L* and promptitude, and looks studied so as to show 'Sallustius.' Nephew and adopted son of the Historian. neither delight at the death of the old Prince nor *who at* excessive sorrow at the accession of the new one, *"meT* did he blend tears with smiles and sighs with compliments. The Consuls Sextus Pompeius and Sextus Apuleius were the first to swear allegiance to Tiberius Ccesar, and then administered the oath to Seius Strabo, superintendent of the Prastorian cohorts, and Caius Turranius, superintendent of the cornsupply. After them the Senate, the soldiery, the people. For it was Tiberius' custom to inaugurate everything with the Consuls, as though the Commonwealth was still a reality and his autocracy open to doubt. Even his summons for the assembling of the Senate he issued only in right of his Tribunician authority, to which he had been raised under Augustus; and the words in which it was couched were few and scrupulously moderate in purport. 'The honours to be paid to his father should be his care. And his place was by the side of the corpse. This was the only public duty which he assumed to himself.' Such were his words. What he did was to issue the watchword to the Prastorian cohorts, as commander-in-chief, the moment Augustus was dead. He had the sentinels, patrols, and all the state of a court. Whether he went to the Forum or the Senate, it was with an armed escort. He sent off despatches to the army without showing any qualms about his succession. It was only in his speech to the Senate that he be-

came at all scrupulous; the chief reason being his fear of Germanicus, who, being master of so many legions and such enormous auxiliary contingents, and the darling of the people, 'Strabo.' Father of Sejanus. might prefer possession to the prospect of sovereignty. Besides this, he so far bowed to public opinion as to wish to seem the choice of a free Commonwealth rather than to have stolen to the throne by a woman's manoeuvres and a dotard's adoption. Another reason came out later. His simulated hesitation was to test the dispositions of the nobility. For he would wrest a word or a look into a crime and then treasure it up for ever. 8. At the first meeting of the Senate he per-*Thewiiuf* mitted no business to be transacted except the *IS?* 'For he would wrest,' etc. Sir Thomas More's character of Richard III. is in many points curiously like the portrait Tacitus draws of Tiberius. Many of his phrases read almost like translations of the language applied to Tiberius in the 'Annals:' e.g.

Free was he called of dispense. Erogandse per honesta pecuniae cupiens.

With large gifts he get him un-Propertio decies sestertium larsteadfast friendship. gitus est. Ceteri silentium et paupertatem confessioni et beneficio prseposuere. None evil captain was he in Spectatum bello. war.

Close and secret. Perinde divina humanaque ob tegens.

A deep dissembler. Abstrusum et tristissima qusque occultantem.

Lowly of countenance, arrogant Adroganti moderatione. of heart.

Outwardly coumpinable where Quanta Tiberii arte gravissimum he inwardly hated. exitium inrepserit dein repres- sum sit, postremo arserit cunctaque corripuerit. Not letting to kiss whom he Honora oratione quse velut exthought to kill. cusando exprobravit. Dispitious and cruel. 'Invidia.' 'Sevitiam super biamque ejus.' 'Suspicacem.' Tacitus's account of Tiberius's reluctance to assume the government, and the embarrassed flatteries of his courtiers may also be compared with Sir Thomas More's account (as reproduced in Shakspeare) of the offer of the crown

to Richard.

final settlement of Augustus's affairs. In the *f.'* will handed in by the Vestal Virgins, Tiberius *Senate on* and Livia were declared heirs. Livia was adopted *obe"* into the Julian House and the Augustan title. *Pfto* o *Augustus.*

As next heirs to the succession he had mentioned his grandsons and great-grandsons, and after them the leading nobility; this being out of ostentation and the hope of getting credit with posterity, as most of them were personally hateful to him.

His legacies were no larger than those of a private

362,500. citizen, except that he left 43,500,000 sesterces to the people and commonalty, to the soldiers of

*si. Gs. 8d.* the praetorian cohorts 1,000 sesterces per man, and to the legionaries and enrolled Roman citizens 2Z. 10. 300 sesterces per man. Next they discussed his obsequies, the most imposing details seeming to be the procession of the funeral through the triumphal gate, proposed by Gallus Asinius, and Lucius Arruntius' proposal to bear in front of the procession the names of the laws which Augustus had carried and of the nations which he had subdued. Messala Valerius brought forward a supplementary proposition to renew the oath to Tiberius every year; and on Tiberius enquiring whether it was at *his* suggestion that he made the proposal, replied that he spoke of his own accord,

« and would not even, at the risk of giving offence, permit himself to become another person's puppet in matters appertaining to the state. This was the only way in which men could now flatter.

By acclamation the Senate voted that the corpse should be borne by senators to the pyre. Cassar

'Vestal virgins.' Temples, and especially temples of Vesta,

were used as depositories for wills, treaties, &c.

deigned to condescend to the concession, and by proclamation cautioned the people against a similar display of affection such as had thrown the funeral of the Immortal Julius into confusion, and against desiring that the body of Augustus should be burnt in the Forum rather than its destined resting-place the Campus Martius. On the day of the funeral the soldiery were drawn up as if on guard, to the derision of those who had seen with their own eyes and whose fathers had told them of that day when their chains were not yet rivetted on them, when they attempted unsuccessfully to regain their freedom, and when the slaying of Julius Ca3sar seemed, if to some men a most infamous, to others a most glorious action;

and now to think that a Prince who was so old,

who had reigned so long, who had furnished his heirs withal with the means of offence against the

Commonwealth, had actually to be guarded by a military escort that he might be laid uninsulted in his tomb!

9. And this gave rise to much personal gossip *Favourable* about Augustus; many people idly marvelling at such coincidences as his accession to the Empire Sept. 1. and his death having occurred on the same day, and his having died in the same house and bedroom at Nola as his father Octavius. Everyone, too, had in his mouth the number of his consulships, six. which were as many as those of Valerius Corvus Seven. and Caius Marius put together; the fact of his tribunician power having been prolonged through thirty-seven successive years; his having won the title of Imperator twenty-one times; and others of his honours which had been heaped on him over and over again, or invented to meet his case. Sensible men commented on his life, some with praise and some with blame. His partisans pleaded filial duty and state-exigency, such as left no scope at that time for the action of the law, in excuse of his appeal to civil war which could by blameless means be neither raised nor maintained. He had made many concessions to Antonius in order to secure the punishment of his father's murderers, and to Lepidus also. When the latter became an indolent dotard, and the former was ruined by his profligacy, the one cure possible for the dissensions of his country was monarchical government. And yet the Commonwealth had been organised not as a Kingdom or Dictatorship, but under the simple title of Prince. TheEUne, The limits of the Empire were the Ocean or reDanube, *i* rivers. One link united everything—the Euphrates. y, the provinces, the navy. The rights of the citizens and the feelings of the allies had been respected. As for the metropolis it had been splendidly embellished. If arbitrary measures had been used, they had been very rare and only to secure the general tranquillity.

10. The opposite party averred that 'filial *pisparag*duty' and 'state exigency' were merely a mask he had assumed; in reality it was his lust of 9sovereignty which induced him to stir up the veterans by bribery, to raise an army, though he was a stripling and of private rank, to tamper with the,Consul's forces, and affect a leaning towards Pompey's party. And later, after a resolution of the Senate had enabled him to usurp the executive and judicial powers of Preetor, after

R.o. 43. Hirtius and Pansa had been slain (and none could tell whether it was the foe had slain them, or whether Pansa's wound had been poisoned and Hirtius murdered by his own men, with Cassar as the instigator of the treachery), he had possessed himself of both their armaments, he had wrung the consulship from the reluctant senate, and the forces which had been entrusted to him against Antonius he had turned against the state: even those who carried out his orders could not eulogise his proscription of the citizens and allotment of estates: true it was that Cassius and the Bruti were sacrificed as his father's foes (though duty demanded that individual animosities should give way to the national welfare), but Pompeius had been deluded by the phantom of peace, and Lepidus by the mask of friendship; later too, Antonius had been ensnared by the treaties of

R.c. 37. Tarentum and Brundisium and by his marriage »-c 40. with Octavia, and the penalty of that treacherous alliance was death; no doubt they had subsequently enjoyed peace, but it was a blood-stained

B.c. 16. peace; there was the disaster of Lollius, the

A.d. 9. disaster of Varus; at home there were the murders of Varros, Egnatii, and Juli. Nor did they refrain from comments on his domestic relations. 'Nero's wife had been ravished from him, and this outrageous question put to the priests whether she might with propriety marry as, though she was pregnant, her child was as yet unborn; there were the excesses of Quintus Tedius and Vedius Pollio; finally, Livia was a baleful mother to the state, a baleful stepmother to the family of the Caesars; they had nothing left to honour the Gods with, when he would be worshipped with the honours of heaven—shrines, busts, flamens, and priests; even Tiberius was not selected as his successor out of affection or a feeling of duty to the state, but, as Augustus had gained an insight into his supercilious and morose disposition, he had aimed at aggrandising his own reputation by a comparison with inferiority.' For the fact was that Augustus a few years previously, when he was demanding a renewal of the Tribune's privileges for Tiberius, though his speech was generally complimentary, yet had let a few hints fall about his manners, tastes, and mode of life which exaggerated under the mask of extenuation. So men talked. Meanwhile, after due celebration of his obsequies, they voted that a chapel should be raised to him with a religious service.

11. But it was to Tiberius that they forthwith *Tiberius* addressed their entreaties. He, on his part, had *show of* some speech ever ready as to how infinite the *thegovem*empire was, how insignificant his own merits, how , none but a superhuman intelligence like that of *9ister read*. Augustus was equal to so tremendous a strain; how he himself, having been summoned by Augustus to share his anxieties, had been taught by experience how laborious, how dependent on circumstances, was the work of superintending everything. For this reason, a state which could command the services of so many distinguished men

ought not to devolve all its burdens on one man's shoulders; the functions of the Commonwealth would be more easily discharged by the division of labour among several people. The sentiments of such a speech were more dignified than sincere; and the language of Tiberius, always, either from nature or habit, equivocal or enigmatic, even in matters which he did not disguise, now, above all, when he was trying his utmost to conceal his sentiments, was shrouded still deeper in vagueness and mystery. Then the senators, whose sole anxiety was to avoid the appearance of intelligence, broke out into wailing and weeping and supplications, stretching out their hands to the gods, to the bust of Augustus, and to Tiberius's knees, as he ordered the register to be produced and read in which was recorded the national wealth, the number of enrolled citizens and allies, of the fleets, kingdoms, and provinces, of the taxes and tributes, of the necessary and voluntary expenditure, all transcribed in Augustus's own hand, and supplemented by a recommendation which it is hard to say whether jealousy or prudence prompted—to confine the Empire within its existing limits. 12. Meanwhile, as the Senate stooped to the *Gallus* most abject protestations, Tiberius casually re-*Tiberius.* marked that, unequal as he felt himself to the management of the whole Commonwealth, he was none the less ready to undertake the care of such a portion as should be assigned him. Whereupon Asinius Gallus observed, 'Would you inform us, Caesar, what portion of the Commonwealth you wish to be assigned you?' Confounded by this startling question, for a moment or two he remained silent; then, recovering his self-possession, replied, that it ill became his humility to select or shrink from any portion of that from which he would rather be relieved altogether. Then Gallus, who had gathered Tiberius's displeasure from his c looks, spoke again, to the effect that the objet of his question was not to sever what was essentially inseparable, but to convict him, out of his own lips, of the indivisibility of the body politic, and the impossibility of its being governed except by a single mind. He went on to pronounce a panegyric upon Augustus and upon Tiberius's own victories, with allusions to his civic achievements during all these years. Not even thus did he allay the Prince's resentment, by whom he had been long detested, from the feeling that, having contracted a marriage with Vipsania, Marcus Agrippa's daughter, once Tiberius's wife,-he was soaring too high for a private citizen, and had not lost the imperious spirit of his father, Pollio Asinius. 13. Lucius Arruntius next gave equal offence *Hateriws* by a speech of much the same tenor as that of *Scaums* Gallus. But against Arruntius Tiberius had no yaw,, grudge of long standing, though he mistrusted him as being opulent, energetic, and as accomplished as he was popular. In fact, Augustus, when, with his dying breath, he was going over the list of those who, having capacity, would shrink from supreme power, or, without capacity, would aspire to it, or would unite ability with ambition, had mentioned Manius Lepidus as able but indifferent to it, Gallus Asinius as ambitious but deficient in abiHty, and Lucius Arruntius as not without qualifications for it, and likely to make a bold stroke for it if any chance came in his way. In the case of the first two there is no dispute. But some have substituted Cneius Piso for Arruntius; and all of them except Lepidus were before long, on different charges concocted by Tiberius, made away with. Quintus Haterius, too, and Mamercus Scaurus, galled his jealous temper: the former by saying, 'How long, Cassar, will you permit the Commonwealth to remain without a head?'—the latter, by the remark, that he saw room for hope that the Senate's entreaties would not prove abortive, in the fact that Tiberius had not, in virtue of his tribunician prerogative, vetoed the motion of the Consuls. Against Haterius, Tiberius launched out at once. Scaurus, for whom he felt an intenser hatred, he passed over in silence; and, being wearied out by the universal importunity and the remonstrances of individuals, gradually yielded so far, not as to own his assumption of the Empire, but as to avoid refusals and solicitations. Haterius, we know, when, in order to apologise, he had entered the Palace, and was grovelling at Tiberius's knees as he was walking, was almost slain by the soldiery because Tiberius stumbled, being tripped up either by accident or by the suppliant's hands. Yet not even this peril to a man of such distinction softened him, till Haterius interceded with Augusta, and at her most pressing entreaties was left unharmed. 14. Great, too, was the Senate's sycophancy to *Tke&* Augusta. Some gave it as their opinion that she *atum of* should be styled parent, some mother, of her country, and a majority that the words 'Son of Julia' *%J* should be added to the title of Cassar. Tiberius, *Tiber iw nomi* insisting that honours must be conferred on *wo-nates* 12 men with discrimination, and that he would prac-/tise the same moderation in the case of such as *f'* should be offered to himself (though he was really distracted by jealousy, and looked on the elevation of a woman as his own disparagement), would not permit her even the privilege of a lictor, and forbad the erection of an altar to commemorate her adoption, and other similar honours. But he solicited proconsular command for Germanicus Caesar, and ambassadors were dispatched to announce his appointment, and also to condole with him in his grief for Augustus's death. Against demanding the same honour in behalf of Drusus, there was the fact that Drusus was Consul designate, and present at Borne. He designated twelve candidates for the praetorship, the number being of Augustus's establishment; and on the Senate's inviting him to extend it, he solemnly swore not to do so. A.d. H. 15. This was the first occasion on which the *motion of* elections f were transferred from the Campus Mar-*TMaus* tius to the Senate, for up to that time, though all those of importance went according to the fiat of *Senate.* the Prince, some were left to the inclination of *stituied in* the tribes. Nor did the people murmur at their *AgtL* rights being wrested from them, save by idle grumbling, while the senate heartily welcomed the gift, because it released them from the necessity of stooping to bribery and beggarly solicitations, and because Tiberius expressed himself satisfied with nominating not more than four candidates, who should be elected without opposition or canvass. At this conjuncture the tribunes of the Commons solicited permission to 'The Proconsular command i.e. in perpetuity. t 'The elections.' Cf. c. 81. Tiberius recommended candidates to the Senate instead of to the people, but the comitia still continued to be held to ratify the Senate's choice. celebrate, at their own expense, games to be called after the name Augustus—Augustales— and enrolled among the festivals. But the expense was charged to the exchequer, and though they might wear the triumphal dress in the circus, permission to ride in a chariot was refused. After a time, the annual commemoration was transferred to the praetor allotted to decide suits between citizens and aliens. 16. Such was the state of things at Eome when *Mutiny of* a mutiny broke out among the troops in Pan-Jjjj nonia, with nothing new to account for it except *Pf Percenmus* so far as the change of sovereign held out im- *the ring*punity to a revolution, and a prospect of profit from a civil war. In the summer-quarters three legions were concentrated under the charge of Junius Bkesus, who, on hearing of Augustus's death and Tiberius's accession, had, for mourning or festivity, let them off their usual duty. It was this which originally led to the soldiers becoming turbulent, quarrelsome, ready to pay attention to all the worst characters, and at last eager for a life of opulence and ease, and disdainful of discipline and toil. There was in camp a man of the name of Percennius, once claqueur-in-chief at the theatre, then a private soldier, glib of tongue, and, from his practice in professional partisanship, skilful in stirring up a crowd. He, in talk with them at night or nightfall, began cautiously to insinuate his influence into their simple minds, which were taken up with canvassing the probable terms of service after Augustus's death, and, as the more respectable dropped off, to gather the scum of the army as his audience. 17. At last, when other abettors of mutiny *sedition* were ready, he would demand, in declamatory "rX style, 'what made them serve as slaves a handful of centurions, and still fewer tribunes? When would they dare to demand redress, if they would not face a novice, still tottering on his throne, with their supplications or their swords? Sufficient their error in having remained passive all these years, so as, grown decrepit and most of them mutilated, to be groaning under their thirtieth or fortieth year of service. Why, even when they had served their time, they were yet not quit of service, but, as supernumeraries, toiled through the same duties under another name? And should anyone, by accident, have escaped with bare life from all these hardships, even then he was dragged away to alien lands, where, under the name of farms, they were presented with swampy fens or mountainous wastes. Burdensome and beggarly enough, in all conscience, was actual service, when life and limb were valued at ten ases a-day; and even out of that they had to provide, not only their clothes, their arms, their tents, but to buy off the brutality of their officers, and their leaves of absence. Yet to these stripes and scars, to freezing winters and scorching summers, to savage wars and starving 'Aput vexillum.' Vexillarii were: 1, men who during the last quarter of their twenty years of service were liable to be called on to fight, but were exempt from the other duties of the legionary. Cf. 36, 39. 2. Soldiers serving under a vexillum of their own, i.e. as a detachment from the main body. Cf. 38. 3. The actual bearers of the vexillum. Vexilum means: 1. A flag. 2. The general's flag on a field of battle. 3. A detachment. worth 16 ases. peace there was no end. Nor was there any cure for all this, unless entrance to the service were placed Then under specified regulations, namely, pay to be a denarius per man, the term of service to be limited to sixteen years, no supernumerary service to be required, but pay to be discharged in cash at the soldier's proper head-quarters. The Prtetorians were paid two denarii per man; after sixteen years they were restored to their hearth-sides. Were the dangers they endured greater? They cast no reflections on those patrol-duties about town, but *they* served among savage nations, and the enemy was in sight at their tent doors.' 18. The crowd applauded from various mo- *Outbreak* tives, some bitterly pointing at scars left by the *fWers.* lash, others at their grey hairs, but most at their *?f J interposes.* threadbare and tattered clothing. At last their frenzy reached such a pitch that they discussed the incorporation of three legions into one. Being deterred by jealousy (for everyone coveted the specific distinction for his own legion), they adopted another plan, planting in a group the three eagles and the colours of the cohorts. At the same time they piled together clods and built up a tribunal to make the position more conspicuous.

In the bustle, Blassus came up, and began upbraiding and checking them, man by man, passionately crying out, 'Sooner than do this, stain your hands in my blood! The murder of an officer may be pardoned; treason to an Emperor, never! While they leave me my life, I will hold my troops to their duty; or if they kill me, it will quicken their remorse!'

19. Not a whit the less quickly went on the *Blew* erection of the mound, and it was by this time *suggests* breast-high, when at length, yielding to his perti- *idiers.* nacity, they desisted from their work. With the consummate tact of an orator, Blaesus said ' that *Tiberius.* the demands of the soldiery must not be an- *His son* nounced to Cassar by mutinous outbreaks, and that their ancestors had never sought such innovations from commanders of yore, nor had they themselves from the Immortal Augustus. Especially inopportune was it to add to the anxiety of one who had hardly commenced his reign. But if they were really determined to require, in peace, what not even the conquerors in the civil wars had demanded, why think of violating their traditional loyalty and the sanctity

of military obedience? They should select deputies, and give them their instructions in his presence.' It was carried by acclamation that
Bkesus's own son, a tribune, should act as deputy,
and should claim for the soldiers discharge after sixteen years' service. Their other demands they would reserve till their first had come to a successful issue. After the young officer had started,
there was comparative quiet. But the soldiery were puffed up by the proof which the son of their general, being spokesman of the common cause, afforded, that they had wrung by compulsion what they would never have procured by milder means.

ober-20. Meanwhile, the companies dispatched to *mmtat*
Laybach. Nrtus previous to the mutiny to see after the roads, bridges, and other requisites, when they heard of the ferment at head-quarters, decamped, *quarter*and, after pillaging the adjacent villages and also *Eu/us!*

Nauportus, which was on the model of a free town, assailed their centurions, as they tried to restrain them, with jeers and insults, and at last with blows; their most violent rage being wreaked on Aufidienus Eufus, prtefect of the camp, whom they dragged from his carriage, loaded with knapsacks, and drove in the front column, ironically inquiring whether such enormous burdens, such prodigious marches were quite to his taste: the fact being that Eufus, who after long service in the ranks had been made centurion and subsequently prasfect of the camp, was for restoring the stern discipline of old times, for being inured to toil and hardships, he was all the more inflexible from having undergone them himself.

21. Their arrival was the signal for a fresh out-*The arrival of the de* break, and in straggling parties they proceeded to *tachment* ravage the surrounding district. Blaesus gave orders *TM* o o D *portus vn* for the flogging and incarceration of a few of them, *fi .. mutiny.* who were heaviest laden with plunder, in order to strike terror into the rest, for even now the centurions and all the respectable men in the ranks obeyed the general. The culprits began to struggle with their warders, grasping at the bystanders' knees, calling out sometimes the names of individuals, sometimes of the century, cohort, or legion to which respectively they belonged, with ever the same outcry that they were all doomed to a similar fate. In the same breath they heaped abuse on the general, invoked Heaven and the powers above; in short, left no stone unturned to work on sentiments of disgust, of pity, of dismay, and of passion. With one accord a rush was made to the rescue, and, breaking into the guard-house, they freed the prisoners, and thus finally identified themselves with deserters and men convicted of capital crimes. 22. From that hour the flame waxed fiercer, and the ringleaders of the mutiny increased in *Vibulenus* number; and a private, named Vibulenus, hoisted "*mLml* on the bystanders' shoulders in front of Blassus' „TM tribunal, addressed the excited crowd flocking to see what he was aiming at, in these words: 'Ah! you have given back light and the breath of life to these guiltless unfortunates, but who gives life back to my brother; who gives my brother back to me? Emissary from the army of Germany to you in our common interests, next night he was butchered by those bravoes of his whom he keeps in arms to prey upon his soldiers. Tell me, Blaesus, where have you cast away his corpse? Even an enemy does not grudge a man a grave. When I have sated my misery with my kisses and my tears then have me slaughtered too, if only my friends here may bury me after I have been murdered for no wickedness but because I advocated the interests of the army.' 23. He lent fire to his words by weeping and *Lueiiius, a* smiting his breast and his face with his hands. *iZ!TM'* Then hurling aside those on whose shoulders he *f* rested, and grovelling in the dust, first at one *h* person's feet and then at another's, he worked *the sth* them up to such a pitch of horror and detestation , that some of the soldiers seized the gladiators f who were bondsmen to Bkesus, some the rest of his slaves, while others dispersed in search of the 'Next night' Or, 'Last night' f 'The Gladiators.' Generals and provincial governors kept gladiators to give entertainments in towns and the camp. corpse. And if it had not soon got wind that no corpse could be found, that the slaves, on being put to the torture, denied the murder, and that Vibulenus never had any brother at all, they would hardly have refrained from murdering the General. They actually did drive out the Tribunes and Prasfect of the camp, ransacked the kits of the fugitives, and murdered the Centurion Lucilius, whom camp wits had christened 'Give me another,' because when he had broken one vine-stick over a soldier's back he would loudly call for another, and then another. The rest escaped by hiding, one only being detained, named Clemens Julius, who, owing to his quick wits, was reckoned a useful medium for communicating the soldiers' demands. Moreover the 8th and 15th legions were on the point of drawing swords on each other, because the men of the 8th clamoured for the blood of a centurion called Sirpicus, while the 15th defended him, had it not been for the soldiers of the 9th, who interposed with entreaties, and against the obdurate with menaces. 24. This intelligence forced Tiberius, reserved *Tiberius* though he was, and the worse the news the more 2TM, likely to hush it up, to despatch his son Drusus J!' *Sejanus to* there with a staff of the foremost men of Eome *the army.* and two cohorts of the Prastorians, not giving him any very definite instructions, but leaving him to take his cue from the circumstances of the case. The cohorts too were reinforced with an extra complement of picked troops. Besides these there was a strong detachment of the Praetorian horse, and the flower of the Germans at that time forming the Emperor's body-guard; and accompanying them the Commander of the Prastorians, iElius Sejanus, who had been appointed colleague of his own father, Strabo, who exercised great influence over Tiberius, and who was to act as counsellor to Drusus's inexperience, and dispenser of rewards and punishments to

the rest of the troops. At Drusus's approach the army, with an affectation of duty, went out to meet him, not with the customary rejoicing nor with glittering standards, but with unsightly squalor and looks indicative of obstinacy, though they feigned contrition. 25. Directly he had passed the lines they made *Dmsus* sure of the gates with pickets, and ordered bodies *Tiberius,s* of armed men to remain in readiness at appointed , positions in the camp. The rest, in a surging multitude, thronged round the tribunal. Drusus was standing and beckoning for silence with his hand. They, as ever and anon they threw a glance at their numbers, broke out into brutal yells, only to tremble again as they looked on Caesar. There was a confused hum, now swelling into a howl of fury, now sinking into a sudden lull. With the sway of conflicting passions they by turns felt and inspired awe. At last in a lull in the hubbub he read his father's letter, the purport of which was that there was nothing nearer his heart than solicitude for those gallant soldiers, his comrades in many a campaign, and the moment his anguish of mind was alleviated he would represent to the Senate their demands. Meanwhile he had sent his son to accord unhesitatingly all that could possibly be conceded at once. All else must be reserved for the Senate, which either in indulgent or vigorous measures should have its proper share. 26. The crowd replied that Clemens, the Cen-*Clemens* turion, had been charged with the delivery of *demandsof* their demands; and he began with 'Discharge ', after sixteen years' service,' 'The rewards to be given on completion of the full term,' 'Pay to be a denarius a day,' 'Exemption of veterans from supernumerary service. '—' Subject to the approval of *Drums re*the Senate and my father,' interposed Drusus, and ffj? was at once howled down with 'Why was he *Senate,* there at all if it was not to increase the soldiers' *which pro* . i.ii i i *duces an* pay, nor to lessen their labours; with no boon *explosion* whatever, in fact, at his disposal? Yet it was left 9at anyone's—aye! anyone's discretion to flog or to execute. Time was when Tiberius used to balk the wants of the soldiers by referring them to Augustus, and now Drusus renewed the same game. Were they never to have any but heirs apparent to visit them? It was passing strange that the interests of the soldiery were the one point referred to the Senate by the Imperator. Why, at that rate, he should take the senate into counsel whenever he issued orders for a punishment or engagement. Must payment be under magisterial supervision, yet punishment be without appeal?' 27. At length they moved off from the tribunal, *Lentulus* as any Prastorian or friend of Caesar's met them, "*ndoniy* menacing him with gestures such as provoke *J* violence and end in blows; exasperated at Lentu-lus more than anyone as he, from his age and renown as a warrior, was supposed to be most resolute in upholding Drusus, and foremost in his scorn for the outrageous excesses of the soldiery. And not long afterwards, as he was setting off with Cassar and because he saw danger ahead, return ing to the winter camp, they closed in on him with a storm of questions, 'Where he was off to

—the Imperator or the Senators?—there also to be the evil genius of the army.' With that they made a rush at him, hurling stones. In a moment he was hit by one and bleeding, and death seemed inevitable when the troop that had accompanied

Drusus ran up and rescued him.

28. Accident made a night so ominous and ripe *An eclipse n i /y , i. l i of the moon*

Sept. 26. tor outrage, pass on quietly; the moon being seen ,, " to lose her brightness, though at the full and in a cloudless sky. This, the soldiers, in their igno-*takes ad*-

ranee of the true cause, took for a prognostic of *au/ruaU*

their present circumstances, comparing the eclipse *d,*

of the planet to their own exertions; and expecting success in their efforts should the goddess be re-instated in her brilliancy and lustre. So with the clash of cymbals and clang of clarions and bugles they raised a noise, exulting or desponding as she brightened or grew dim. And when the gathering clouds hid her from their gaze, and they believed that the darkness had swallowed her up, with all the credulous superstition of minds once unstrung they fell to bemoaning the ills without end in store for them, and the frown of Heaven that was on their enterprise. By order of Drusus, who was minded to make a wise use of fortune's favours, the round of the tents was gone,

and the Centurion Clemens summoned with any others who by honourable means had ingratiated themselves with the common soldiers. They mixed with the watches, pickets, sentinels of the gates, and allured or alarmed them with promises or threats, 'How long is the siege of the Impe-

rator's son to last? What is to be the end of the struggle? Is it of Percennius and Vibulenus that we mean to swear ourselves the men? Will Percennius and Vibulenus lavish pay upon the soldiers, land upon the veterans? Are they, we say, instead of the Drusi and the Neros, to grasp the government of Eome? Had we not better be the first to show our sorrow, as we were the last to go astray? What all demand is granted grudgingly. To ensure priority of indulgence there should be priority of claim.' With such words filling their minds with anxiety and mutual jealousy, they set the young soldiers against the veterans, legion against legion. And so, gradually, the instinct of obedience revived. The gates were abandoned. The standards, which at the outbreak of the mutiny had been all grouped together, were restored to their respective positions.

29. At daybreak Drusus called an assembly *A deputa*and, though an unpractised speaker, yet with in-*mrifJ* stinctive magnanimity upbraided them for their f£ former conduct, applauded them now; declared that no threats or intimidation could move him, but that if he saw them submissively yielding, and heard the language of entreaty, he would write to his father that it would please him to take the petition of the army into consideration. At their re-

quest the same Bkesus who went the first time, Lucius Apronius, a Eoman knight of Drusus's suite, and Justus Catonius, a senior centurion, were despatched to Tiberius. Then there arose a conflict of opinion, as some recommended waiting for the ambassadors, and mean while mollifying the soldiery by conciliation, others a recourse to a more drastic treatment. 'With the rabble there could be no half-measures. If not terrified they were terrible. Once overawed they could safely be despised. While they were still under the influence of superstition, the general should strike fresh terror by putting the ringleaders of the mutiny to death.' Stern measures were most congenial to Drusus. He sent for Vibulenus and Percennius and ordered them for execution. According to the common report they were buried in the General's tent; according to others their corpses were cast outside the entrenchments for an example. 30. The next step was to hunt up all the most *The other* », i-i. *ringleaders* notorious mutineers, some oi whom, while strag-*put to* gling beyond the camp, were slain by the centurions or privates of the Pratorians; while even ' the companies gave some into custody as a guarantee of their loyalty. The distress of the soldiers had been aggravated by a premature winter, with such incessant and violent storms of rain, that they were unable to leave their tents or assemble together, and could barely keep the standards upright against the fury of the wind and rain. Still also were they haunted by awe of Heaven's wrath, and the thought that those paling stars and pouring tempests were no purposeless menace to evildoers; that nothing could rescue them from their misfortunes but departure from this ill-omened and accursed camp, and, after expiatory sacrifices, the return of everyone to his respective winter-quarters. The 8th legion went back first. The 9th had loudly demanded that they should stay for Tiberius's letter; but after a while, as the others filed off, and they found themselves isolated, they did betimes voluntarily what they must soon have done perforce. And Drusus,

without awaiting the return of the embassy, satisfied that the storm had blown over for the present, went back to Eome.

31. On nearly the same days, and for the same *Simui*reasons, disturbances arose in the army of Ger-*outbreak of* many—the more outrageous in proportion to its *'fQTM* greater numbers, and because they confidently expected that Germanicus Caesar would not be *Cmcma.* able to brook another's supremacy, and would place himself at the disposal of the army, which would thus become sole master of the situation. On the banks of the Ehine were two divisions, one called the Upper, commanded by Caius Silius, while Aulus Caecina was in charge of the Lower; Germanicus being the commander-in-chief, and at the time engaged in collecting the tribute of Gaul. Now the division of Silius, with wavering resolution, watched the fate of mutiny elsewhere; while the men of the lower division abandoned themselves to a paroxysm of fury, which originated with the 21st and 5th legions, and spread to the 1st and 20th; for they still occupied their summer-quarters Near on the frontiers of the Ubii, either with nothing ' at all or but very little to do. So, on hearing of Augustus's death, the swarm of slaves lately After the enrolled at Eome, lawless in their habits and imoTvarus Pi f work, began poisoning the simple minds of their comrades with 'Now was the hour for the old soldiers to insist on early discharge, the younger on more liberal pay, and all alike on some

D limitation of their hardships, and revenge for the brutality of the centurions.' No single malcontent here, like Percennius among the troops of Pannonia, nor among soldiers who trembled as they listened and eyed askance other and stronger armies, but tongues and mouthpieces of mutiny in abundance. 'In their hands lay the destinies of Eome; theirs were the conquests which aggrandised the Commonwealth; the Imperators were affiliated to titles which *they* had won.' 32. They met with no check from their Officer, *Massacre* for their fury and their numbers had un-

nerved *fJ+££* him. All at once they rushed madly, with drawn swords, upon the centurions, the immemorial *dered to* object of the soldiers' abhorrence, and mark for *ncersby* the first burst of outrage. Sixty at each of them, *chorea* so as to correspond to the centurions' number, *y* they threw them down and cruelly beat them, and *f* then cast them, mutilated and mangled, and some *saUants.* of them dead, either in front of the entrenchments or into the Ehine. Septimius, who had fled to the tribunal, and was grovelling at Caecina's feet, they yelled for incessantly, till he was delivered to his doom. Cassius Chasrea, who in aftertimes made his name for ever memorable by killing Caius Cassar, being at that time in the vigour of youth and of dauntless spirit, hewed a road with his sword through the weapons of his antagonists. And now no authority could be asserted any longer either by Tribune or Prasfect of the Camp.

'Immemorial object.' I am aware that the English does not adequately convey the force of the Latin which seems to defy translation. Principium has a mixed meaning: 1, that the centurions were the cause; and, 2, the victims of mutiny.

Pickets, outposts, and whatever else the exigencies of the moment suggested, the mutineers proceeded to distribute among themselves. To the more attentive observer of the temper of the soldier, this was the clearest indication of a wide-spread and obstinate ferment, that not separately, or at a few persons' instigation, but as one man they flamed into fury, as one man were mute, with such perfect uniformity and regularity, that you might fancy it was at the word of command.

33. Meanwhile Germanicus, engaged, as I said, *Germani*in collecting the tribute in Gaul, received intel- ligence of the death of Augustus, whose grand-*%%£!'* daughter, Agrippina, he had married, and had by *twemiivia* her a number of children, besides being the son of *wife.* Drusus—Tiberius's own brother—and grandson of Augusta. Yet he was harassed by the covert antipathy of his grandmother and uncle, the motives

for which were all the more venomous because unjust. For the fact was, that the Eoman people retained a strong affection for the memory of Drusus, and he was supposed to be meditating the re-establishment of freedom if he should have succeeded to power. And this created towards Germanicus a similar liking and reliance; for he was a young man of winning disposition and re 'Winning.' Civilis is an epithet applicable to a man who behaves as one citizen should to another. It does not admit of exact translation. 'Popular,' 'public-spirited,' 'sociable, ' 'gracious,' 'unpresuming,' 'good-natured,' 'constitutional,' etc., all convey something of what is meant by 'civilis,' which, according to the context, leans towards one or another meaning. Cf. cc. 54, 72, etc., and also Milton's' The Reason of Church Government against Prelaty.' 'To inbreed and cherish in a great people the seeds of virtue and public civility.' markable affability, strongly in contrast to the cold, dark looks and language of Tiberius. He was also involved in the squabbles of women—Livia actuated by all a stepmother's rancour towards Agrippina, and Agrippina herself somewhat too irritable. Only her chastity and affection for her husband guided even her imperious temper to a good end. 34. But Germanicus, in proportion as he arrived *He comes* nearer to the height of his ambition, set himself £" to strive all the more earnestly in behalf of My *received.*

Tiberius, imposing on himself, his suite, and the Belgian cantons, the oath of allegiance to him. Afterwards, immediately on hearing of the ferment in the army, he came in haste, and found them outside the camp, from their downcast looks apparently contrite. Directly he had passed the lines, a hum of discontent became audible, and some, grasping his hand, under pretence of embracing it, pushed his fingers in so as to feel their toothless gums; while others kept pointing at their limbs, bowed by old age. Seeing the absence of all order in the assembled crowd, he gave the word to 'form companies.' 'They could hear better where they were,' was the reply. 'At all events, to marshal themselves behind their colours, that there might be some means of distinguishing between the cohorts.' Doggedly they did so. Then, after a prefatory tribute of respect to Augustus, he diverged to the conquests and successes of Tiberius, especially applauding his most brilliant exploits in the Germanies with those very legions. Next he flatteringly alluded to the unanimity of Italy, the loyalty of Gaul, the absence of all turbulence and disaffection everywhere. They listened to him either in silence or with stifled interruptions.

35. As soon as he touched on the mutiny, *Heup*again and again appealing to them, 'What had JjJ./ become of their submission as soldiers, what of *goffer him the* the discipline that was once their boast, what they *Empire,* had done with their tribunes, their centurions?' *though* to a man they tore off their clothes, and bitterly fjsfjf. pointed at scars of wounds and weals of the lash. *f . status*

Then, with tumultuous cries, they reviled the *sneersat* dearness of exemptions, the niggardly pay, the *f acting.* severity of the service; and (specifying them by name) the lines, the entrenchments, the foraging for provisions, timber, firewood, and all the other contrivances, either imperative or to prevent the soldiers having nothing to do. Sternest of all swelled the cry of the veterans, with their catalogues of thirty and more than thirty years' service, adjuring him to have mercy on worn-out men, and not doom them to work, work on, until they dropped dead, but grant them cessation from such oppressive service, and rest that should not be beggary. Some of them also claimed the sum left them by the Immortal Augustus—a claim of happy augury for Germanicus—and proffered their services should he desire to reign. Then, indeed, as if polluted by their wickedness, he leaped at a bound from the tribunal. They barred egress with their weapons, and insisted, with menaces, on his going back; while he, with passionate protestations that he preferred death to disloyalty, snatched his sword from its scabbard, raised it aloft, and was plunging it into his breast, had not those nearest him caught and forcibly held his hand.

The most remote part of the assemblage, and, what is hardly credible, some individuals stepping up closer, pressed him ' by all means to strike home;' and a soldier of the name of Calusidius drew his sword and offered it, recommending it as being sharper than Germanicus's own. Ferocious though they were, this seemed too brutal and inhuman; and the pause which followed allowed Caesar's friends to carry him off to his tent.

36. There they deliberated what was to be *He debates* done. For it was reported that an embassy was *Ziuhe* being organised to induce the Upper Army to make common cause with the Lower; that the *plans of* town of the Ubn was doomed for destruction; *neen.* and that the troops when once inured to plunder would run riot in the pillage of Gaul. To add to their alarm there was the enemy aware of the mutiny and certain to attack should the bank be left unguarded, while to arm the contingents and allies against the mutinous legions was to embark on a civil war. To be rigorous was dangerous, and it was degrading to give way. Whether everything or nothing were yielded to the soldiery the commonwealth ran an equal risk. So, after consultation as to their policy, they resolved to indite in Tiberius' name a letter authorising the discharge of those who had served twenty years; the disembodiment with liability to supernumerary service, but exemption from all except defensive duty, of those who had served sixteen; and as to the legacies claimed, that they should be doubled and paid. 37. The soldiery perceived that these offers *He grants* were made to gain time, and insisted on their peremptory fulfilment. The discharge was hurried *charge,*

on through the medium of the Tribunes. Pay-*misestut*

ment was postponed till they were at their res-*jf*

pective head-quarters. But the men of the 5th *y*

and 21st legions would not move from

the sum-*winter* mer quarters where they were, till the money was Tjt/im made up out of the travelling fund of Germanicus and his friends, and paid in full. The 1st and ff" _ *being paid* 20th legions were led back by their officer Caecina *at once.* to the canton of the Ubii, the column to its shame *leads part* marching with the Imperator's private treasure *the* carried among the standards and colours. Ger-*Vbumter-tory. Crer* manicus proceeding to the Upper Division im-*manicus* ii i *n* l i *n* l l *ff* posed the oath of allegiance on the 2nd, loth, and *Upper* 16 th legions without any opposition. On the part *the* of the 14th there had been momentary hesitation, *oathof* and without their demanding it they were offered *allegiance.* their pay and discharge. Between 38. Meanwhile among the Chauci some draughts *Mutiny of* ancUhT fr the mutinous legions on garrison-duty com-*numZy* Elbe. menced an outbreak, but were for a time quelled by the prompt execution of two soldiers. Manius Ennius, Praefect of the Camp, was responsible for *Manius* this order, which was rather effective as a deterrent *represses* than justifiable by law. By and by, as the ferment ' swelled higher, he fled but was discovered, and as he found no safety in hiding, trusted to boldness to bear him through. 'Their outrages were offered, not to a Prefect but to their General Germanicus, to Tiberius their Imperator.' With that, overawing those who barred his way, he seized the flag, faced round to the river, and loudly declaring that he would hold any man who dropped out of the column as a deserter, led them back to their winter quarters, disaffected but dismayed.

39. Meanwhile, commissioners from the Senate *Theut* reached Germanicus, who by this time had r&-*Legions at* Bonn(?) turned to the altar of the Ubii. With him, in *zTM* winter-quarters, were two legions, the 1st and TM 20th, and the lately disembodied supernumeraries. *Caipur*Panic-stricken, conscience-stncken, they were seized *Mm.* with apprehension lest the commissioners were come instructed by the senate to annul what they by their mutiny had extorted. And as a mob must always throw the blame on some one, however unfairly, they charged the chief commissioner Munatius Plancus, an ex-consul, with having drawn up the Senate's ordinance; and in the dead of the night set up an outcry for the flag kept in Germanicus's quarters; and with a rush at the gate forced the doors, roused up Caesar from his bed, and compelled him by menaces of death to give up the flag. Soon afterwards, as they straggled along the camp-streets, they came full upon the commissioners, who on hearing the alarm were hastening to Caesar, loaded them with insults, and were on the point of murdering them, especially Plancus, who had thought it beneath him to resort to flight. In this jeopardy he had only one asylum open to hiin— the camp of the 1st legion. There he stood clasping the standards and colours, trusting their sanctity would be his safeguard. And had not the standard-bearer Calpurnius saved him from the worst of their violence, the blood of a commis 'Disaffected but dismayed.' Cf. c. 42. Or the words may mean, 'their courage broken and not having dared to strike one blow.' sioner of the Eoman people would have stained the altar of the gods in a Eoman camp, a thing of rare occurrence even among foes. At last, at daybreak, when it was possible to distinguish officers, soldiers, and what was going on, Germanicus coming into camp ordered Plancus to be escorted to him, and set him at his side on the tribunal. Then inveighing against their infatuated madness, rekindled by what he called the anger, not of men but of the gods, he explained the object of the commissioners' arrival; pathetically dilated on the inviolability of an ambassador, and on the gross and unprovoked maltreatment of Plancus, and withal the blackness of the stain thrown on the honour of the legion; and while the assembly stood surprised rather than sat-isfied, he sent the commissioners away under an escort of auxiliary horse. 40. As things were so threatening, Germanicus *Germani*was universally condemned for not proceeding to H" the Upper Division, where obedience and aid fHr'" against the mutineers was ready to hand. 'He «"»y- , *sends away* had blundered enough, and more than enough *Ms wife* already, with his discharges, largesses, and policy ", of conciliation. But, if he recked nothing of his personal danger, why expose a little son, a pregnant wife, to the mercy of madmen and outragers of humanity? Them, at all events, he ought to restore to the boy's grandfather and to the state. ' At last, after long hesitation and tearfully clasping to his bosom her and the son of their love, he forced her to leave him; though she indignantly begged him to remember that she was of the blood of Augustus, and no craven to shrink from danger.

Slowly it set out, this sad procession of weeping women, she the general's wife, and yet a fugitive with her little boy upon her bosom, their friends' wives, subject to the same constraint, wailing around her, while the distress of those they left behind was not less poignant.

41. This spectacle, which was not of a Prince *Remorse* in prosperity or in his own camp, but such as is seen in a conquered city, along with the moaning and lamentations, attracted the notice and attention even of the soldiers. Out of their huts they trooped. 'What meant that sound of weeping? Why thus dismally were these high-born ladies— not a centurion, not a soldier to escort them—and with none of the state or retinue to which an Imperator's wife was entitled, going to trust themselves to the Treviri and the honour of foreigners?' With that came a revulsion of remorse and pity, and the recollection that she was daughter of Agrippa, granddaughter of Augustus, daughter-inlaw of Drusus; how fruitful she had been as a mother, how stainless as a wife; then of her child too, born in the camp, reared in the huts of the army, whom in rough soldier-phrase they had dubbed ' Caligula,' because, in order to win pop-

ularity, he generally wore that kind of shoe. But what chiefly moved them was jealousy of the Treviri. They crossed her path with entreaties to return, to stay with them, some of them running in Agrippina's way, most turning back to Germanicus. He on his part, still glowing with indignation and resentment, commenced this harangue to the surrounding throng: 42. 'To me wife or son is not dearer than my *Speech* sire and the state. He, however, will be guarded *Germani*by the grandeur of his position, the realm of Borne , by her other armies. My wife and my little ones, whom gladly I would devote to destruction to enhance your renown, as it is I withdraw beyond the reach of your frenzy, so that, be your wicked intentions what they may, they may be satisfied with my blood only, and that the murder of the great-grandson of Augustus, the butchery of the daughter-in-law of Tiberius may not make you more guilty than you are. For from what insolence or sacrilege have you shrunk during all these days? What name am I to give to this assemblage?" Soldiers" must I call you, you who have beset the son of your Imperator with entrenchments and with arms? or "citizens," after you have set at nought the majesty of the Senate?

'Why what even an enemy respects, the inviolability of ambassadors and the law of nations, that you have trampled on! The Immortal Julius quelled his mutinous soldiers with one word, by addressing those who were for renouncing his service as "civilians." The Immortal Augustus cowed the army of Actium with a glance and a frown. And if I, who though I am not yet what they were am none the less of their blood, should be treated with contumely even by the soldiers of Spain or of Syria, it would be an astounding scandal. And is it by you, by the 1st legion, to which Tiberius presented its colours, by the 20th, his comrade in so many battles, the recipient of so many favours, that this splendid return is rendered to your General? Is this the intelligence I am to take to my sire as he listens to none but good news from the other provinces? how his own recruits, his own veterans are dissatisfied with their discharge and with their pay; how here, and here only, are centurions massacred, Tribunes chased away, ambassadors mobbed, a blood-stained camp, blood-stained rivers, and myself amid men craving after my life, preserving it only by my prayers!

43. 'Ah! why, why on that first day's assem-*Speech* blage, 0 too thoughtless friends, did you turn " aside the weapon which I was about to plunge into my breast? A truer and trustier friend was he who offered me a sword. I should at all events then have died unconscious as yet of these multiplied enormities of my army. The General whom you would have elected, though he might have left my death unatoned for, would have avenged the death of Varus and his three legions. Forbid it, Heaven, that Belgians, though voluntarily coming forward, should achieve such glorious renown as to have rescued the honour of Eome and quelled the tribes of Germany! Immortal Augustus! let thy blest spirit, let the vision, let the recollection of thee, Drusus! with these self-same soldiers, who even now are touched with remorse and generous feeling, wipe away this stain, and wash out the quarrels of brothers in the slaughter of the foe! You too, whose altered looks and altered feelings I perceive, if you would give back to the Senate its commissioners, to your Imperator obedience, to me my wife and son, shrink away from the others and leave them to their disaffection. That will be a pledge of your penitence, a bond for your loyalty.' 44. Melted by his words, and owning his re-*lite* proaches were just, they implored him 'to punish the incorrigible, pardon those who had been mis-*Zdemn* led, and lead them against the foe; to bid his *TM£* wife return and give back to them the child of the *chief muti neers.* army, and not hand him over a hostage to the Gauls.' He urged against Agrippina's return her approaching confinement and the severity of the weather. His son should come. As to punishment, they must see to that themselves. Away they hurried in all directions, no longer the same men, and dragged in fetters all the ringleaders of the mutiny before Caius Caetronius, the officer of the 1st legion, who pronounced sentence on each of them, and carried it into execution in the following manner. The legions, with drawn swords, stood before the Eostrum. The accused, in custody of a Tribune, was placed in full view on an elevation. If the shout was 'Guilty,' he was immediately thrust down and cut to pieces, while the soldiers gloated over the bloodshed as though they thought it washed away their own guilt. Nor did Caesar interfere, for, as he had given no orders, they alone were responsible for the ferocity of the act, as well as for the abhorrence it would excite. The veterans followed this example, and were soon afterwards despatched to Khaetia, nominally to protect the province from the Suevi, who were threatening it, really to hurry them away from a camp now become terrible as much from the rigour of the punishment as from recollection of the crime. Germanicus then reviewed the centurions, each of them at the Imperator's summons stating his name, rank, and native country, the number of his campaigns, his feats of prowess in battle, and, if he had any, his military distinctions. Whoever was certified to be assiduous and steady by his Tribune and legion kept his rank. Whenever he was unanimously charged with cupidity or cruelty he was dismissed the service.

45. After thus quelling the mutiny in his own camp there was still in store for him a not less *pares to* arduous task, owing to the turbulence of the *force the* 5th and 21st legions, who were in winter quar-*TMhand*

BirtenTM- P Vetera, sixty miles off. Xanten. *Yov* they had been the first to mutiny, and by *Xantm.* their hands all the most frightful atrocities had been perpetrated. Unawed by the punishment, uninfluenced by the contrition of their comrades, their rancour remained unabated. So Caesar prepared to send down the Ehine arms, ships, and a force of allies, resolved, should they continue contumacious, to appeal to the sword.

46. Meanwhile at Rome, where as yet they *Alarm at* were ignorant how things

might have issued in *Murmurs* Illyricum, intelligence of the outbreak in the army of Germany frightened the citizens into invectives against Tiberius ' for befooling such helpless, weaponless puppets as the Senators and people with his assumed hesitation, while all the time the soldiers were in open mutiny and not to be quelled by a couple of striplings as yet too young to enforce obedience; it was his duty to go in person and overawe with his august presence men who would at once give way when brought face to face with a Prince of such practised capacity, who was at once the sole dispenser of strict punishment and liberal reward. Could Augustus in the decrepitude of old age make progress after progress into Germany, and ought Tiberius in the vigour of life to loiter in the Senate, carping at the language of the Senators? He had taken enough precaution for the slavery of civilians, let him apply a sedative to the temper of the soldiers, and render them peaceable and contented.' 47. To all such strictures Tiberius opposed an *Tiberius,* inflexible resolution not to quit the Capital, nor im peril his person and the State. There were, really, *p%* many perplexities to embarrass him. The army *however, to* 01 (iermany was the strongest, lhat ot rannonia *person to* was the nearest. The former was backed up by , the resources of Gaul; the latter was at the threshold of Italy. To which, then, was he to give the preference? Would he not in any case exasperate by the affront those who were set aside? Whereas through the medium of his sons both were alike accessible, and his dignity, which distance made more imposing, was uncompromised. Besides, such youths would be pardoned for referring some points to their father, and those who might disobey Germanicus or Drusus could be conciliated or crushed by himself. But what else was there to appeal to if the Imperator were once treated with disrespect?' However, as if always on the eve of setting out, he selected his suite, provided his equipage, fitted out a fleet; then, by alleging sometimes stress of weather, sometimes press of business, he imposed at first even on the shrewd, still longer on the masses, and on the provinces longest of all. 48. Meanwhile Germanicus, though he had cOn-*Germani'* centrated his forces, and was taking steps to punish S" the mutineers, thought he ought still to leave *notice to* them a chance of profiting by the lesson so lately *wtatthf* taught them, and sent a despatch to advise Caecina *TM* ' *may expect.* that he was coming with a strong force, and that, *y* unless they should previously punish the guilty, *and mashe* would put them indiscriminately to the sword. *theJm*This despatch Caecina read privately to the colour-*p*bearers, ensigns, and the best affected portions of the men, imploring them to rescue the whole army from dishonour and themselves from death. For, though in time of peace motives and services were taken into consideration, under the pressure of war the guiltless and the guilty fell side by side. They, after sounding those whom they judged the likeliest men, and finding the greater part of the legions true to their duty, according to their Officer's wish, fixed a time for an onslaught, sword in hand, on all the most flagrant and disaffected of the mutineers. Then, at a preconcerted signal, they made a rush on their tents and cut them to pieces, taking them by surprise and without anyone save those in the secret knowing what was the origin of the massacre, or what would be its end.

49. Of all the fighting between fellow citizens *Germani* ,1,1-1 i. *cus comes* that ever happened, none ever assumed an aspect *to the camp* like this. Not in battle, not from hostile camps, £ but rising from the same bed, those who had fed - mli-ii i i-i-i *fitst cam* side by side by day, and slept side by side by *paign* night, divided into two bodies, and commenced a "*Germans* discharge of missiles. The cries, and wounds, and bloodshed were palpable to all. The cause was a mystery. The issue was as chance disposed it. Some also of the well-affected were killed when, on its becoming clear who were the objects of this furious assault, the criminals in their turn had snatched up weapons. There was no commander, no tribune to control them. Eiot and revenge and carnage stalked abroad unchecked. After a time Germanicus came into camp, and exclaiming, with a flood of tears, that this was not a remedybut a butchery, ordered the bodies to be burnt.

And now, still thirsting for blood, they were seized with a longing to march against the foe who should be the sacrifice for their frenzy; for the only way to appease the spirits of their comrades was to bare their guilty bosoms to honourable wounds. Cassar fell in with their martial ardour, and throwing a bridge across carried over twelve thousand of the regulars, twenty-six cohorts of the allies, and eight squadrons of cavalry, whose discipline had been preserved inviolate throughout the mutiny. 50. The Germans were full of exultation, and *He defeats* were not far off, while we were kept inactive by the public mourning for the death of Augustus, and afterwards by our dissensions. But our general by a forced march cleared a way through on the the Caesian forest, and the barrier which Tiberius ofthe had raised, and pitched his camp in the latter, reen *the* fortifying himself in front and rear by a rampart, Lippe and the flanks by a barricade. Starting from this the Kuhr. point he penetrated the maze of forest-passes, 'Forest-passes.' Saltus cannot be translated by any single word. As used in these books it seems always to mean some pass through woods. Such words as 'glade ' do not give its meaning. Of. cc. 51, 60, 63, II. 11, 14. In II. 11, Saltus is used of a place where the huge shields of the Germans and their long spears could not be wielded as easily among the trunks of trees and brushwood as the pila and sword and close-fitting armour of the legionary. Cf. also with this I. 68

E deliberating whether of two routes he should take the direct and frequented one, or the one more intricate and unexplored, and consequently unguarded by the foe. Deciding on the more roundabout route, he hurried on everything else as fast as possible. For scouts had reported that that night was a festival with the Germans, consecrated to mirth and revelry. Caecina received orders to push on ahead and clear away the obstructions of the forests. The legions followed at no great distance, a bright starlight night was in their favour, Near and they reached the settlement of the Marsi, and posted pickets round them while they were still stretched on their beds or at the tables, under no apprehension, and with no sentinels on the look out. So utterly careless and disorganised were they at all points and unsuspicious of an assault. And even their repose was merely the stupid torpor of intoxication. 51. Caesar, in order to extend the range of his *Destnc*ravages, divided his eager legions into four *m/ana.* columns and laid the country waste for fifty miles *ff* with fire and sword. Neither sex nor age excited -, *bantes, ana* compassion. The property of men and of gods, *Wpetes.* and even the shrine, far-famed among those nations, and called by them Tamfana, were all alike levelled to the ground. The soldiers had not received a wound, for those they had slain were half asleep, unarmed, or straggling. This On the carnage stirred up the Bructeri, Tubantes, and On the Usipetes, and they beset the forest-passes through " which the army had to retire. Germanicus, hearing this, advanced ready to march or fight. In the van were some of the regular cavalry and the cohorts of the allies; after an interval came the 1st legion. The baggage was in the centre, and was flanked by the 21st legion on the left, the 5th on the right. The 20th formed the rearguard. Eearmost of all were the rest of the allies. The enemy, till the column was winding through the passes of the forest, remained motionless, then keeping up a skirmish with the flanks and van, broke with full fury upon the extreme rear. And the light cohorts were being thrown into disorder by the swarming masses of the Germans, when Caesar galloped up, and in his loudest tones repeatedly cried, 'Now is the hour for wiping out the mutiny. Forwards! Onwards! Turn your guilt into glory!' Their souls took fire, and with a rush they broke through the enemy,

drove them back into the opening and put them to the sword; and at the same moment the troops of the vanguard emerged from the forest and threw up entrenchments. After this, their march was unharassed, and the soldiers, emboldened by their late exploits to forget the past, went into cantonments for the winter. 52. This intelligence filled Tiberius with *Tiberius* i mi *recounts* pleasure and also jealousy. Ine suppression of the mutiny was most welcome, but it tormented him to think of Germanicus having won the affections of the soldiers by lavishing pay and *fdai praise* expediting their discharge, and of his having *matZus,* gained such military renown. Yet he brought TM his conduct under the Senate's notice, and pro-*p? f Drusus.* nounced on him a glowing eulogium in language too pompous to be thought heartfelt. More briefly he expressed his approval of Drusus *achievements to the Senate with arli* and the termination of the mutiny in Ulyricum, but with greater earnestness and in words that were sincere. He also confirmed all the concessions of Germanicus to the forces in Pannonia as well. 53. In the same year Julia breathed her last, / having been confined for unchastity by her father *Murder of* s. Maria. Augustus first in the island of Pandateria, after
Eeggio. wards in the town of the Ehegini, who live by the Straits of Sicily. She had been the wife of Tiberius while the prospects of the Caesars, Caius and Lucius, were still unclouded, and had looked down on him as beneath her in rank. And this was Tiberius's strongest motive for retiring to Rhodes. When he had succeeded to the sovereignty, while she remained an exile and in disgrace, and after the murder of Postumus Agrippa a prey to despair, he got rid of her by leaving her to pine away by starvation; thinking that from 15 years, the length of her banishment her death would pass unnotieed. He had similar reasons for implacability against Sempronius Gracchus, a man of high rank, shrewd intellect, and perverted eloquence, who had debauched this same Julia when she was the wife of Marcus

Agrippa. Nor did his profligacy end here. When she had been given to Tiberius, this insatiate libertine inflamed her with disobedience and disgust for her husband, and the letters full of vituperation of Tiberius which Julia wrote to her father Augustus were supposed to be the composition of Gracchus. For
Kerkine. these reasons he was banished to Cercina, an island in the African sea, where he languished in exile for fourteen years. When the soldiers came to put him to death they found him on an eminence on the shore, boding no good from their visit. When they came, he begged for a brief respite to enable him to communicate by letter his last wishes to his wife Alliaria, and then bowed his neck to his executioners, in his death evincing a fortitude not unworthy of the name Sempronius, which he had dishonoured during his life. According to one account, the soldiers were not sent from Eome, but by Lucius Asprenas, proconsul of Africa, at the instigation of Tiberius, who had idly imagined that the opprobrium of the murder might thus be shifted to Asprenas.
54. The same year witnessed the establishment *College of* of fresh rites, and a new college of priests of the *'ur o/* fellowship of Augustus, according to the precedent ", furnished by Titus Tatius, who, to preserve the Sabine rites from oblivion, had founded the Titian *the rivalry* Brotherhood. Twenty-one of the great men of ƒEome were selected by lot, Tiberius, Drusus, Claudius, and Germanicus being the additional members. The Augustal sports which were then inaugurated were disturbed by the squabbles of the actors. Augustus had countenanced this entertainment out of regard to Mascenas, who was a passionate admirer of Bathyllus. And he was himself by no means averse to such amusements, and considered it politic condescension to mix with the diversions of the populace. Tiberius's inclinations were of another sort, but as yet he did not venture to mould to sterner habits a people humoured with such indulgences during a number of years. 55.

In the consulship of Drusus Cassar and *Germani*Caius Norbanus, a triumph was decreed to Ger-*cits pre*manicus, though the war was still going on. fi" Early in the spring, he anticipated the summer campaign (though he was preparing to prosecute it with vigour) by a sudden swoop upon the *Rivalry of* Hesse. Chatti; for he had become hopeful that the *ant"* enemy was split into fractions for Arminius and Segestes, who were respectively famous for treachery and loyalty to our rule. Arminius was the firebrand of Germany. Segestes often warned Varus of the impending insurrection, both on other occasions and at the banquet immediately preceding its outbreak, and advised him to arrest himself and Arminius and the rest of the chiefs; for if deprived of their leaders, the people would lose all heart, and he could at his leisure investigate who were guilty, who innocent. But Varus was doomed to fall, and by the sword of Arminius. Segestes, though forced into the war by the unanimity of his nation, continued disaffected, his personal irritation being exasperated by the fact of Arminius having carried off his daughter, though she was betrothed to another man. The son-in-law was detested by the father-in-law, and reciprocated his hatred, and what with friends are the ties of affection became the fuel of animosity to foes. were blended together, and everything everywhere looked ominous for the Eomans; the ground with its bottomless swamps which gave way if they stood still, and was slippery if they advanced; the weight of mail on their bodies; their inability to hurl their pila. The Cherusci on the other hand were used to fighting in fens, being long of limb and with huge spears capable of inflicting wounds even at a distance. At length, night saved the legions, which were already giving way, from defeat. The Germans in their success feeling no weariness, without taking any rest even then, set to work to turn over the lowlands all the waters rising in the surrounding highlands, and by flooding the ground and washing away such work as had been completed forced the soldiers to toil through it all over again.

Forty years' service had Cascina seen either as private or officer, and his experience of prosperity and peril made him dauntless. But though he thought over possibilities, he could hit on no other plan than to pen the enemy within the wood, till the wounded and the encumbered part of the column were well ahead. For half-way between the hills and fens there was a level plain large enough to admit of a line of battle on a small scale. The legions selected were the 5th for the right wing, the 21st for the left, the 1st to form the vanguard, the 20th to face the foe in the rear. 56. On these considerations Germanicus handed *Germani*over to Cajcina four legions, five thousand auxiliary *pJofhu* troops, and the irregular levies of the Germans west *?.* of the Ehine, and marched in person at the head of . ii-i *the* an equal number oi the regular legions and twice *cherutd* as many allies. And after building a fort on the *TheAiarst* site of his father's entrenchments, on Mount Taunus, with his army in light marching order, *flying corps*
he swooped upon the Chatti, leaving Lucius *mand*
Apronius in the rear, to keep up his communications by road and river; for, as is seldom the case in that climate, owing to the drought and shallowness of the water-courses, he had not been impeded in his swift march, and the rainstorms and the rise of the rivers were to be dreaded on his return. But he took the Chatti so completely by surprise that all those who were helpless, either from age or sex, were made prisoners or cut to pieces at once. Their ablebodied men swam across the Adrana, and attempted to prevent the
Eomans from constructing a bridge. But being driven off by the engineers and bowmen, and after in vain endeavouring to arrange a peace, some of them deserted to Germanicus, and the rest,
abandoning their villages and hamlets, scattered in all directions into the forests. Caesar, after burning Mattium, the capital of the canton, and ravaging the open country, faced about to the Bhine, without the enemy venturing to harass the rear of his retreat, as their

custom is when they have retired by way of stratagem rather than from fear. The Cherusci had intended to aid the Chatti, but Caecina, by the celerity of his movements in all directions, scared them away,
and kept the Marsi in check by winning a battle in which they had ventured to engage.
57. Not long afterwards, emissaries came from *He relieves*
Segestes, entreating protection from the violence *fndc%-*
of his countrymen, by whom he was beset, owing S»/
to Arminius, as the advocate of war, having supe-*rminius.*
rior influence; for, with barbarians, the bolder
and more energetic a man is, the more trustworthy and eligible is he esteemed in stormy times. Segestes had attached his son Segimundus to the emissaries, but thoughts of the past made the young man hesitate; since, in the year of the insurrection of Germany, when he had been consecrated priest at the altar of the Ubii, he had rent the garlands and fled to the insurgents. Induced, however, to rely on the mercy of Eome, he did his father's behests, and was graciously received, and sent to the Gallic side of the river, under an escort. This made it worth while for Germanicus to countermarch, and he fought a battle with the beleaguering force, and rescued Segestes, with a large body of relatives and dependents, including some women of rank. Among them was the wife of Arminius, who was also daughter of Segestes, but showed the spir it of her husband rather than her father, letting not a tear bespeak her weakness, nor an appeal for pity leave her lips, but keeping her hands clasped tight upon her bosom and her eyes fixed upon her pregnant womb. Trophies of the catastrophe of Varus were also brought in, having fallen to the lot of most of those who now gave in their submission; and along with them Segestes, in person of commanding stature, and exhibiting all the fearlessness of a faithful ally. 58. His words were to this effect:—' Not for *Segestes's . speech to* the first time

to-day do I display unswerving *Germani*loyalty to the Eoman people. Since the Immortal "/Wif-"'' Augustus presented me with the franchise, I have chosen my friends and my foes with a view to your interests, and not out of malignity to my fatherland (for traitors are loathed even by those they serve), but because I hold German and Eoman interests to be identical, and peace to be preferable to war. This was the reason I denounced to Varus, who was then General, this ravisher of my daughter, this outrager of your treaty, Arminius. Thwarted by the torpor of that commander, and as I could place but scant reliance upon the laws, I earnestly begged him to arrest Arminius and his accomplices, and myself. That night—would to Heaven it had been my last —be my witness that I speak the truth. What happened subsequently is indefensible, and can only be deplored. What *I* could do I did. I threw Arminius into chains, and endured the same degradation myself at the hands of his partisans. And now, when for the first time I can side with you openly, I prefer what is ancient to innovations, and tranquillity to turmoil; and this, not from venality, but to clear myself from treason, as well as to be an appropriate mediator for the German nation, should it prefer penitence to perdition. I entreat your indulgence for the youth and indiscretion of my son. I admit that nothing but compulsion has brought my daughter here. It must rest with you to deliberate which should weigh most with you — her being the mother of the child of Arminius, or my child herself.'

Caesar replied graciously, assuring him of safety Germany for his children and relations, and of an establishment for himself in the old province. He then 'When for the first time,' etc. Or the words may mean, 'When you can protect me, ' or, 'when you give me the chance.' led his army back, and, by order of Tiberius, received the title of Imperator. Arminius's wife gave birth to a son, who was brought up at Eavenna, and whose after story and the insults of which he became the butt, I shall subsequently relate.

59. The report of the surrender and gracious a *harangues* reception of Segestes was greeted with hope or *hucoun* .,.. . *trymen* indignation, in proportion as people were averse *against the* to or eager for war. Arminius, always of a fierce temper, was driven frantic by the capture of his wife and the fate of his unborn son foredoomed to slavery, and was ever in motion among the Cherusci, calling for war against Segestes, war against Cassar. And he did not refrain from insults. 'A perfect Father, a mighty Imperator, a valorous army, to have carried off, with a myriad hands, one weak woman! *Be* had made three legions, three Generals, bite the dust; for he waged war, not by treachery, nor against pregnant women, but face to face against armed men. To this hour might be seen, in the groves of the Germans, the Eoman banners, which he hung up in honour of the gods of his fatherland. Segestes might settle on the conquered side, might reestablish his son in the priesthood of men! With Germans nothing could atone for the symbols of Eoman law and the garb of Eoman citizens having been seen between the Ehine and the Elbe. Other nations were undefiled by Eoman punishments, uncompelled to pay Eoman imposts, because they were unacquainted with Eoman rule; but they who had felt it and spurned it, and sent back from a bootless errand that hero of theirs, Augustus, ranked among the Immortals, that hero of theirs, Tiberius, the man of their choice, would surely never cower before an inexperienced stripling and a mutinous army. Let all who loved their fatherland, their fathers, and the old life better than servitude and strange settlements, choose Arminius as their leader to fame and freedom rather than Segestes, to the infamy of the slave.'

60. By such language not only were the Che-*Rising of*
rusci but the adjacent tribes stirred up, and Inguiomerus, Arminius's uncle, whose influence with *f*
the Eomans was of long standing, was drawn over *through the*
in *Bructeri to* to his side. This mcreased

Caesar s anxiety; and, *the Ems.* to prevent the whole fury of the war bursting on *ueamiry* him at once, he despatched Caecina, at the head of *fZ* forty Roman cohorts, through the country of the *f n f'*
Ems. Bructeri, to the river Amisia, to effect a diversion *tier. Ger* of the enemy. The cavalry were led by their *Ztth/ltr* Friesiand. Commander Pedo along the Frisian frontier.

Caesar in person, embarking with four legions, *f* Zuyder-conveyed them through the lakes, and a simul-*Zuyder-Zee* taneous junction was effected by the infantry, *Ems at its* cavalry, and fleet, at the river fixed as the rendezvous. The Chauci proffering their aid, were enrolled in the service. Lucius Stertinius, detached with a flying force, routed the Bructeri, who were laying their own lands waste; and, amid the carnage and pillage, he came upon the colours of the 19th legion, lost with Varus. The line of march then led to the extreme limits of the Bructeri, and all the tract of country be*Lippe.* tween the Amisia and the Lupia was laid waste, Between almost up to the forest-pass of Teutoburg, in
Pader-which the remains of Varus's legions were said to born and 1 r
Osnaburg. he unbuned.

61. And this filled Caesar with a longing to *The bones* perform the last rites to those soldiers and their *"u* general; and all the army with him was to a man melted by compassion for some kinsman or friend, or for the calamities of war in general and the ills of humanity. Caecina was sent ahead to reconnoitre the intricate forest-passes, and to span with bridges and causeways the swampy fens and treacherous bogs. In this way they drew near that gloomy spot, as hideous in its appearance as its associations. In Varus's first camp the circumference of the lines and the extent of the central court evinced the handiwork of three legions. Farther on in lines half in ruins, and a shallow entrenchment, the last survivors of the shattered army were conjectured to have made a stand. In the centre of the field their bones lay bleaching, strewn about or in heaps as they had fled or

stood at bay. Near them were fragments of weapons and limbs of horses; hard by, skulls nailed to the trunks of trees. In the adjacent groves were those inhuman altars at which they had immolated the Tribunes and Senior Centurions. And survivors of the massacre, who had escaped from the battle or from bondage, would tell the tale how this was the place where the officers fell; that where the colours were taken; how here Varus was first wounded; and here with a suicide's desperate hand rushed on death; how on yonder rising ground Arminius haran 'The central court.' The ' Principia ' was to the camp, what the Forum was to a town. gued his men; how all those gibbets and those pits were for his prisoners; and how in his wantonness he insulted the standards and the colours. 62. And thus it fell out that six years after the *msappro*massacre, this Eoman army, sadly and sternly, with vows of deeper vengeance against the foe, buried in one common burial, as if all were of their own kith and kin, the bones of the three legions, no man knowing whether it was a stranger's remains or those of his own relations that he was committing to the tomb. At the raising of the barrow Caesar laid the first sod, duly doing honour to the departed, and out of sympathy with the sorrow of the living; an act disapproved by Tiberius, either because he put a bad construction on everything Germanicus did, or because he imagined that the vision of their massacred and unburied comrades must damp the ardour of the army for battle, and make it more fearful of the foe; and that it was unbecoming in an Imperator, in whom was vested the augurate with its most venerable functions, to pollute his hands with the arrangements of the tomb. 63. But Germanicus followed Arminius in his *indecisive* retreat into the wilds, and at the first opportunity ordered the cavalry to deploy and scour the plain TM£TM occupied by the enemy. Arminius, who had-£'»»""'« urged his men to form m masses, and keep in the *cm re-em*vicinity of the woods, wheeled round suddenly, *saihdown* and presently gave the word to those whom he *lna'*

had kept concealed in the forest-passes, to rush '"' out. The cavalry were thrown into confusion by *Bridges* these fresh antagonists, and the cohorts sent to *that At*
Ksevorden.
their aid, being carried away by the flying rout, *minim has* had increased the panic, and were only saved *f* from being driven into a morass familiar to their conquerors but disadvantageous to men unacquainted with it, by Cassar's bringing up the legions and forming them in order of battle. This struck terror into the enemy and reassured our men; and the combat ended without decisive results. Soon afterwards he led back the army to the Amisia and brought them back, as he had come, by ship. A division of the cavalry was ordered to strike the Ehine by route of the seacoast. Cascina, who was in command of an independent force, was urged, though he was familiar with the line of his retreat, to waste no time in Near getting to the other side of the Long Bridges. This was a narrow causeway in the heart of a wilderness of morass, constructed in times past by Lucius Domitius. All around it was bog, with quagmires of clayey mud or invisible waterbeds, encircled by gradually sloping forests which were then occupied by Arminius. For he had got ahead of our soldiers, encumbered as they were with their baggage and arms, by short cuts and quick marches. Cascina, in perplexity whether it was possible to repair the bridges which were old and worn out, and meanwhile keep the enemy at bay, determined to encamp on the spot, in order that while some were fighting others might proceed with the work. 64. The barbarians in their attempts to storm *cadna u* the outposts and assault the men at their work, *f* harassed and surrounded and charged them. The shouts of the workmen and the warriors 65. For both armies it was a sleepless night, *stateofthc* but for different reasons: the barbarians at their revels making the hollow vales and re-echoing "g-, dells ring again with songs of triumph or shouts *dream.* of menace; in the Eoman camp flickering fires, *Second* faltering voices,

and the men lying all along the entrenchments or roaming about the tents in wakefulness rather than watchfulness. And their general had a ghastly dream. He thought that he saw Quintilius Varus bespattered with gore and rising out of the swamp, and that he heard, as it were, his voice calling him, but that he did not follow it and thrust away his outstretched hand. At break of day the legions posted on the wings, either from cowardice or perversity, abandoned their post, hastily taking possession of a field beyond the marshes. Yet Arminius, though they laid themselves open to his onset, did not dash out at once. But when the baggage was floundering in the mud, the men in confusion around it, the array of the banners broken, and as usual at such a moment, everyone in selfish hurry, with ears deaf to their leaders' orders, he gave the word to the Germans to dash at them, shouting again and again, '"lis another Varus, and another army to share Varus' doom.' With that, he and a chosen band hewed a gap through the column, dealing blows mostly at the horses. They, staggering in their own blood and the slippery swamp threw their riders, overturned all in their way, and trampled on the fallen. Eound the colours the struggle raged fiercest. They could not be bor-ne up against the storm of javelins nor planted in the slough of mud. Caecina, while cheering on 'The slippery swamp ':—
'How in the slippery swamp of blood Warrior and war-horse reeled.'
Macaulay's ' Battle of Regillus.' his men, went down, his horse shot under him,
and was only saved from being taken prisoner by the 1st legion throwing itself in the way. The greed of the enemy came to his aid, as in their haste to plunder they ceased to slay; and at nightfall the legions struggled out on open and firm ground. But their misfortunes were not yet over. There were entrenchments to be thrown up, materials to be procured for an earthwork.
Most of the tools for turning up earth or cutting sods were lost. There were no tents for the companies, no dressings for

the wounded. As they shared their food bespattered with blood or mud, they bemoaned themselves for the death-like darkness, and the day that for so many thousand men must be the last.

66. A horse happened to break its halter, and *Panic* running loose and scared by the uproar knocked *Tomans*. down some men who came in its way; which excited such a panic-alarm of an onslaught of the Germans, that everyone rushed headlong to the

Facing the gates, mostly making for the Decuman as being " out of the enemies' way and safer for flight. „

Cascina on ascertaining the alarm to be groundless, and yet being unable to stop or stay the soldiers by his commands or entreaties, or even force, threw himself full length in the gateway, and as their feelings forbad them trampling on the body of their commander, at last succeeded in barring their egress. "Whereupon the Tribunes and Centurions satisfied them that it was a false alarm.

67. Then having called them together to head-C&cina,s quarters, and ordered them to attend in silence to *s*what he had to say, he impressed on them their critical position. They had nothing to rely on but their valour, which however must be tempered with discretion, and they must keep behind their lines till the enemy, confident of storming them, came nearer; then presently they must sally out at all points and by that outburst make good their way to the Ehine. But if they fled, other forests, fens more fathomless, foes no less fierce awaited them; while if they conquered they won honour and renown. He appealed to their domestic affections, to their soldierly pride. He said not a word of failure. When he had ended, he distributed the horses, his own first, then those of the officers and tribunes, without any favouritism, to all the bravest of the soldiers, that they first, and then the infantry, might charge the foe.

68. The Germans were kept in an equally rest-*Arminius'i* less state by their hopes, their cupidity, and the conflicting opinions of their leaders; Arminius JS recommending that they should not oppose their *flight. The* enemy's escape now, but surround them again in *victorious.* other swampy and entangled spots; Inguiomerus's plan being more sanguinary and such as barbarians love, to invest the fines sword in hand, as they could easily carry them, and so secure more prisoners and uninjured booty. Acting on this, at daybreak they trampled in the edges of the trenches, filled them with hurdles, clutched at the parapets, while scarcely any soldiers showed themselves on the summit, such as did being seemingly paralysed by terror. Just as they were scrambling up the fortifications, the cohorts received the signal, and the bugles and clarions sang out.

Then, with a shout and a rush, they poured out upon the rear of the Germans with taunting cries, 'Here were no woods or swamps but fair fortune and a fair field.' The enemy deeming them an easy prey and a handful of half-armed men, were overwhelmed by the clang of clarions and flash of arms, the shock being all the greater because it was a surprise; and they fell fast, as unwary in misfortune as they had been overweening in success. Arminius left the fight unscathed, Inguiomerus badly, wounded. The slaughter of their followers went on while there was fury enough and light enough to slay. At last night came, and the legions drew off weak with many additional wounds, and as destitute of food as they were before, but finding strength, health, plenty, everything in victory.

69. Meantime, the rumour had spread that the *Agnp*army was cut off, and the Germans were in full *duct at this* march upon Gaul, and, unless Agrippina had forbidden the destruction of the bridge built over the Ehine, there were cowards bold enough for that baseness. But during those days this highspirited woman played the part of a general, and dealt out clothing and bandages to any soldier who was wounded or in want. The historian of the German wars, Caius Plinius, relates that she stood at the head of the bridge praising and thanking the legions on their return. This sank deep into Tiberius's mind. These were not, he brooded, disinterested attentions, nor solicitations of the soldiery against any foreign foe. The Imperator might throw up his office, when a woman took to inspecting the legions, issuing the watch-, words, dabbling in bounty, as if there had not been more than enough cajolery already in parading the General's son in a private's uniform, and permitting the Caesar to be called Caligula. Agrippina had more influence with the army than Officers or Generals. A woman had quelled a mutiny, which the name of the Prince was im potent to restrain. Such suspicions were ever in flamed and exaggerated by Sejanus, thoroughly comprehending, as he did, Tiberius's disposition, and sowing seeds of jealousy long to germinate and spring up all the stronger at last. 70. Meanwhile Germanicus, out of the legions which he had brought by sea, put Vitellius in charge of the 2nd and 14th to march by land, *duem*so as to lighten the fleet either for riding over *manf*the shoally sea or grounding at ebb-tide. In *eredt*o the first part of his march Vitellius found no diffi-*TMiTMg* culty, the shore being dry under foot, or only slightly submerged by the tide. Afterwards, *drowned* when a gale from the north blew, and it was, *%e*. besides, the season of the equinox, when the tides rise highest, the order of the march was at an end. Even the land was inundated. Sea, shore, and land, all wore one aspect, and there was no distinguishing what was insecure from what was firm, what was shallow from what was deep. Waves overwhelmed them, whirlpools swallowed them up. Beasts, baggage, lifeless bodies floated about and blocked their way. The companies were all jumbled together with the water sometimes breast-high, sometimes up to the face, and occasionally, when no bottom could be found at. all, were immersed or drowned. As the remorseless wave rolled on, the General's voice and the encouragements of comrades were alike without avail. The courageous and the craven, the wise and the unwary, those who trusted to fore-

thought and those who trusted to fortune, fared all alike. Each and all were swept away by the same irresistible flood. At last Vitellius struggled out to higher ground and helped the column up to the same position. They bivouacked without necessaries, without fire, some of them naked or maimed, in as wretched plight as men beleaguered by a foe. For *they* might at least die a glorious death, but these must die without glory. With the light, dry land reappeared, and they succeeded in reaching the river Visurgis where Caesar had arrived with the fleet. The legions were then embarked, while rumour reported them drowned, nor was their safety credited till men saw Caesar and the returning army with their own eyes. 71. By this time Stertinius, who had been sent *Submission* in advance to receive the submission of Segimerus, Segestes' brother, had escorted both him and his son to the canton of the Ubii. Both were par-y ff doned, Segestes readily, his son less so, because *Germani*he was said to have wantonly insulted the corpse *Idndnessto* of Quintilius Varus. As for the losses the army had sustained, Gaul, Spain, and Italy vied in making them good with proffers of all they respectively had ready to hand, arms, and horses, and money. Commending their zeal, Germanicus only accepted arms and horses for the war, relieving the soldiers out of his own funds; and, in order to render their recollections of their disaster less harrowing, he went the rounds of the wounded, complimenting individuals for their special feats, examining their wounds, and by appealing to one's man ambition, another man's honour, to all alike by his affability and attention, he strengthened their enthusiasm for himself and for the war. 72. That year triumphal distinctions were voted to Aulus Caecina, Lucius Apronius, and Caius *title 'Pater* Silius for services under Germanicus. The title ' of Father of his country, so often thrust on him, Tiberius declined. Nor would he allow any oath of observance of his ordinances, though the Senate voted it; his invariable excuse being the instability of all human affairs, and the greater precariousness of his footing the higher he rose. Even thus, however, he gained no credit for public spirit, for he had revived the law of treason, which, as a name, was of old origin, but had taken cognisance of quite other cases, such as treachery in a soldier, rioting in a civilian, lastly, maladministration of office—acts of high treason against the majesty of the people of Eome. For his actions a man was responsible, but he might say what he pleased. Augustus was the first to strain the letter of this law to prosecution for defamatory libel, being provoked by the outrageous. conduct of Cassius Severus, in having caluminated high-born persons of both sexes in scurrilous lampoons. His successor Tiberius, on Pompeius Macro inquiring whether trials for treason were to be revived, replied that the laws must be enforced. He, like Augustus, was exasperated by the dissemination of anonymous verses, lashing his inhumanity, his arrogance, and his squabbles with his mother. 73. It will not be uninteresting to recount the *Prosecu* and Eubrius, two Eoman knights in easy circum-*and* stances, in order to explain whence this most deadly scourge originated, with what consummate craft Tiberius fanned it into life, and how, for a while, it was smothered, only at last to burst into a blaze shrivelling up everything before it. An informer accused Falanius of having admitted among the votaries of Augustus, such as existed in every family in a sort of brotherhood, an actor called Cassius stained with odious vices; and of formally disposing of a statue of Augustus along with some gardens he had sold. Eubrius was charged with sacrilege in having sworn falsely by Augustus's divinity. On Tiberius being notified of it, he wrote to the consuls 'that this was not why his father had been enrolled among the gods, to make that distinction instrumental to a citizen's ruin. Cassius the actor had been accustomed, along with others of his profession, to act a part in the spectacles which his mother had dedicated to Augustus's memory, and it was no sacrilege that Augustus's statue, like the figures of other deities, should be included in the sale of an estate and house. As for the oath, it must be regarded in the same light as perjury to Jupiter. Insulted Heaven would be its own avenger.' 74. Not long afterwards Granius Marcellus, *Prosecu*Praetor of Bithynia, was arraigned for high treason *Junius* on the deposition (supported by Eomanus Hispo) of his own quEestor, Caepio Crispinus, who entered on an avocation, afterwards rendered notorious by the calamities of the age and men's shamelessness. For, by pandering to the Prince's harsh nature with backbiting calumnies, this beggar, upstart, and busybody, gradually constituted himself the terror of all the most distinguished citizens. The influence he gained over one man gained him the detestation of every one else; and he set a fashion, the imitators of which, though out of poverty they grew rich, and out of insignificance formidable, yet after ruining other men, ended by ruining themselves. His specific allegation against Marcellus was the use of injurious expressions about Tiberius, a charge impossible to repel when the accuser selected the vilest traits in the sovereign's character, and put them in the mouth of the accused. For the expressions were taken for granted merely because they were so true. Hispo further charged him with exalting his own statue above Cassar's, and with having cut off the head of one of Augustus and put the figure of Tiberius in its place. At which Tiberius was so exasperated, that, breaking his silence, he exclaimed ' that he would himself give in his verdict in this case, openly and upon oath,' so as to force the rest to do the same. Even at that time some sparks of expiring freedom still lingered, so Cneius Piso spoke out, 'In what order, Caesar, will you vote? First,.1 hope, so as to give me my cue; not last, for fear I should unintentionally vote the other way.' He winced at this; and in proportion to 'Harsh.' Sssvus is a favourite word with Tacitus. Cf. Saevitia annonae. It is often hardly possible to give its full force by one English word. It has something of the meaning of the old word 'fellon.'
'The battle there sae fellon was.'

Barbour's *Battle of Bannockburn*. The passage might be translated 'by crawling into the good graces of a cruel master.' the imprudence of his ebullition was the forbearance with which, in his regret, he permitted the acquittal of the accused on the charge of high treason. As for the charge of embezzlement, it was referred to the court of recovery.

75. Not satisfied with the courts of the Senators *Tiberius's*
he would take his seat at the trials on the Praetor's *mike*
bench, but at one end, so as not to oust him from *u'of*
the curule chair, and under his auspices many »»«««.
decisions were given in the teeth of intrigues and solicitations of people of influence. But his care for impartiality was the canker of freedom. Pius Aurelius, for instance, a senator, preferred a complaint that his house was made unsafe by the pressure of the high road and an aqueduct, and appealed to the senate for compensation. On the commissioners of the treasury opposing the claim,
Cassar stepped in and awarded Aurelius the price of the house, for he liked to be liberal in deserving cases, a good trait which he preserved when he had lost all others. He made a present of a
8,333 6 8 million sesterces to Propertius Celer, ex-praetor, who pleaded poverty as an excuse for withdrawing from his order, on its being ascertained that his father had left him a poor man. Others who ventured on the same experiment he ordered to substantiate their plea before the Senate, his excessive strictness making him harsh even in his good actions. As a consequence, everyone else preferred silence and indigence to exposure and relief.

76. In the same year, the Tiber, swollen by *Overflew of* incessant rains, swamped the low-lying part of the cbJT, town. Buildings and bodies were borne in havoc away by its ebb. So Asinius Gallus proposed to *pointed to* consult the Sibylline books. Tiberius refused, in *AchaL* '" religion as in politics alike practising reserve. ' But Ateius Capito and Lucius Arruntius were *Procon* deputed to devise means for banking the river in. *suiar and* On Achaia and Macedonia protesting against their *under the* imposts, it was decided they should be relieved *admini*from pro-consular government, and put under Caesar's control. Drusus, in presiding over some *brutality* gladiatorial shows given jointly in the name of his *atorial* brother Germanicus and himself, gloated over the ' bloodshed in a way which, dregs though it was, seemed excessive; a symptom of ominous import to the people, and said to have been reproved by his father, whose own absence from the exhibition was accounted for by all sorts of conjectures, such as ' his dislike to a crowd,' or ' his sombre tastes,' and ' his fear of being contrasted with Augustus,' who used to be a most gracious spectator. That he put in his son's way a temptation to display his savage tastes and provoke the disgust of the people, I should think scarcely credible, though that *was* alleged to be his motive. 77. Meanwhile the riots in the theatre, which *Fresh* had commenced in the immediately preceding *f* year, broke out more violently, several civilians and soldiers and one centurion losing their lives, *menu to* and a tribune of the cohort of Praetorians being *case.* wounded in represssing insults to the magistrates, and the strife of the rabble. This riot was brought under the notice of the Senators, and their decision was pronounced for empowering the praetors to flog actors. Haterius Agrippa, tribune of the people, tendered his veto, for which Asinius Gallus made an attack on him in his speech, though Tiberius remained dumb, true to his policy of amusing the Senate with those phantoms of freedom. However, the veto held good because the Immortal Augustus had on a previous occasion pronounced that actors were not liable to the lash, and Tiberius was not at liberty to contravene his decisions. Numerous enactments were passed to limit their salaries and to check the extravagance of their partisans, the most noteworthy being that no Senator should enter a play-actor's house, no Eoman Knights should escort them when they appeared in public, or witness their performances anywhere except in the theatre; and that the praetors should be empowered to punish by banishment the excesses of the spectators. 78. The Spaniards asked and received permis-*Spain* sion to erect a temple to Augustus in the colony *temple to* of Tarragona, thus setting a pattern to all the pgf' provinces. On the people begging for remission /?«. -. . *remission* of the one per cent, tax on vendibles, which dated *of the* i *per*
» *CBfit tax* from the civil wars, Tiberius announced that the *Tiberius's* funds of the army depended on that impost, and a that even as it was, the State would sink under the rff *"l tisnes the* expense, if veterans should receive their discharge *old term* before they had served twenty years. In this *for the* way the ill-advised discharge, after sixteen years' service, which had been extorted in the late mutiny, was rescinded for the future.

79. The next discussion of the. Senate was on *Debates in* the proposition of Arruntius and Ateius, to draw *about di*off the rivers and lakes which swell the Tiber, in order to abate its inundations; and audience was given to deputations from municipalities and colonies, the Florentines petitioning against the
Chiana. diversion of the Clanis from its proper channel
Amo. into the Arnus, and their own consequent ruin;
Temi. the people of Interamna urging similar objections, to wit, the certain desolation of the richest plains
Nera. of Italy, if the Nar, as was proposed, should be split up into a number of canals and cover the
Eieti. country with a swamp. The people of Eeate also had their grievance, 'protesting against damming
K di up Lake Velinus at its point of efflux into the Nar, for otherwise it would inundate the surrounding district. Nature had made the wisest provision for human interests in fixing the proper mouths, channels, sources, and exits of rivers; some respect also was due to the religious feelings of allies who had consecrated to the rivers of their fatherland, sacrifices, groves, and shrines. Father

Tiber himself would, they well knew, disdain to flow in diminished grandeur when robbed of his tributary streams.' Whether it was the entreaties of the colonies, or engineering obstacles, or religious feeling that prevailed, they carried Piso's . proposal, who had declared himself opposed to change.

80. Poppasus Sabinus's term of government in *meriu'»* Mcesia was extended, and Achaia and Macedonia ££KL were also placed under his charge. This was *commands.* another of Tiberius's customs to prolong commands and keep most men till the end of their lives in the same military or civil appointments. As to his object, every sort of account is given. Some say the repetition of trouble was distasteful to him, and so when he had once made arrangements he perpetuated them; others that it was his malignant spirit, confining the honour to as few as he could. Others again are of opinion that his selections were as diffident as his disposition was astute. For as, on the one hand, he did not look out for conspicuous capacity, so, on the other, incapacity was his abomination. From excellence he apprehended danger to himself, from inferiority discredit to the state. And this irresolution so grew upon him in the end that he appointed to provinces persons whom there was no chance he would ever allow to quit Eome. 81. As to the form which the consular elections JjJESUC took, then for the first time in that, and after-*elections at Borne.* wards in successive reigns, I can assert nothing *How* positively, such conflicting statements occur not *influenced* only in historians, but in Tiberius's own speeches. , At one time he would withhold names of candidates but indicate each individual's family, career, and military service, so as to make his identification easy; at another, withholding even such an inkling, he would impress on the candidates that they should not complicate the election by intrigue, pledging himself to use his own influence in their interest. In general, he declared that those whose names he had proposed to the Consuls were the only ones who had sent in their claims, and anyone else might do the same, provided he could only rely on his popularity or his deserts. A plausible sentiment, but at bottom meaningless or insincere, and in proportion to its more elaborate assumption of the form of freedom certain to find vent in the more grinding tyranny. BOOK II.

A.D. 16, 17, 18, 19.

1. In the consulship of Sisenna Statilius and *Troubles in* Lucius Libo, disturbances arose in the realms and *onones,* Eoman provinces of the East, the movement ' r ' *successor,* originating with the Parthians, who, though at *unpopular* their own request Bome had given them a king, *Parthians.* treated him with disdain as an alien, though he was of the blood of the Arsacids. His name was Vonones, and he had been given as a hostage to the Eomans by Phraates. For Phraates, though he had driven before him Eoman armies and Eoman generals, had shown every mark of reverence for Augustus, and had sent him some of his children in order to secure his friendship, not so much from dread of our power, as distrust of the loyalty of his own countrymen. 2. Phraates died, and as there was nothing but *How Von* ii-i-'i It i *ones had* bloody civil war under his successors, an embassy *obtained* came from the Parthian chieftains in quest of *of* Vonones as his eldest son. This Caesar considered '» *popularity.* highly honourable to himself, and loaded Vonones with presents. The barbarians also gave him a hearty welcome, as is usual at a change of ruler. But soon they were seized with shame 'at the degeneracy of the Parthians, in having gone begging to another world for a sovereign, who was withal corrupted by the education of their foes. Both by repute and in practice, the throne of the Arsacids was, like any other dependency, fallen into the gift of Eome. Were they so dead to those deeds of glory, the extermination of

Crassus, the overthrow of Antonius, that this chattel of Cassar's, this tame slave, through all these years should lord it over Parthians?' By his own conduct also he inflamed their disdain, departing from the customs of his ancestors, seldom going hunting, taking small interest in horses, lolling in a litter whenever he made a progress through the towns, and looking superciliously on the national banquets. His Greek retinue also was their laughing-stock, and his habit of having the most worthless articles of common use stamped with his signet. Even his accessibility and easy condescension, qualities never deemed good by Parthians, seemed bad innovations, so that his virtues and his vices, because alien to their own habits, excited equal detestation.

3. So Artabanus, who was of the blood royal *jrtahanus* Dahistan. and had grown to manhood among the Dahse, was proclaimed, and though routed in the first *who flies to* engagement, recruited his forces, and made him-*state of* self master of the Parthian kingdom. The van-*ArUmL*quished Vonones sought an asylum in Armenia, *Ataxias.* at that time in a state of anarchy, and not to be relied on as an adherent either of Parthia or Eome, in consequence of the crime of Antonius, who by counterfeiting friendship had entrapped Artavasdes, king of the Armenians, then loaded him with fetters, and ended by putting him to death. His son Artaxias, whose affection for his father made him our mortal foe, found a shield for himself and his kingdom in the power of the Arsacidas. He was assassinated by his kinsmen, and Tigranes being appointed to Armenia by Caesar, was, under the escort of Tiberius Nero, put in possession of his sovereignty. Tigranes, however, did not reign long, nor did his children, though they observed the barbarous custom of intermarriage and joint sovereignty. 4. By order of Augustus, Artavasdes was next *Artams*raised to the throne, but was deposed, and not *AHobarz*without disastrous consequences to us. This caused the appointment of Caius Cassar, to adjust *VmoM is . raised to* the affairs of Armenia, and he set up Ariobar-*the throne,* zanes, by birth a Mede, whose extreme personal *into the* beauty and brilliant ability made the appointment a most popular one with the Armenians. When he had been accidentally killed, they refused to

submit to his children, and after trying the experiment of a female sovereign, named Erato, whom they soon deposed, being irresolute, disorganised, and in a state of anarchy rather than freedom, they placed the wanderer, Vonones, upon the throne. But as Artabanus was assuming a threatening attitude, and Vonones had but scant support in Armenia, while if we came to his aid it would entail a war with the Parthians, the governor of Syria, Creticus Silanus, sent for him and kept him in durance, though he retained the pomp and title of a king—an indignity from which I shall in due course relate Vonones' efforts to escape. 5. Tiberius, for his part, was by no means *Tibtrius* displeased at this accidental embroilment of the affairs of the East, as it furnished him with a pre- *tunUyof* text for severing Germanicus from the legions GeTMfa«fwith which he was familiar, and for exposing him Xaraw at once to treachery and failure by appointing ƒhim to a strange province. Germanicus, however, *Plan of the latter* in proportion to the increase of his soldiers' en-*for a third* thusiastic attachment, and the malevolence of the Pintentions of his uncle, grew the more eager to press on to victory, and pondered over his proper tactics and his own successes or reverses in warfare, during an experience now extending to three years. In pitched battle or a fair field the Germans were worsted. Their strength lay in forests and morasses, in the shortness of the summer, and the earliness of the winter. His own men suffered not so much from wounds as from long marches and loss of weapons. Gaul was exhausted with supplying horses. A cumbersome baggage-train was easily surprised, difficult to defend. Whereas by sea a sudden descent was easy for them, impossible for the foe to detect, besides his being able to commence the campaign earlier, and convey his army along with its commissariat; while both horse and horsemen, by means of the river-mouths and channels, would be deposited in the heart of Germany unscathed. 6. To this, therefore, he directed his efforts. *He collects* Dispatching Publius Vitellius and Caius

Antius to *Jf* collect the imposts from Gaul, he gave the build-*vir* ing of a fleet in charge to Silius and Anteius and *Hon* at the Caicina. A thousand ships were reckoned suffi-*"he Satavi.* cient, and were hurried on, some of them being " short, tapering at stem and stern, but broad 'Tapering at stem and stern,' etc. Cf. Motley's description G amidships, so as to resist the waves better; some flat-bottomed, so that they might ground without damage; a considerable number with rudders fore and aft, to enable the rowers, by sharply shifting their oars, to steer ahead or aback as they pleased; many with decks, on which they might carry the enginery, and also equally well adapted for the conveyance of horses or stores; all alike handy under sail, speedy with oars, and rendered the more imposing and formidable by the enthu-

Betu-we. siasm of the troops. The island of the Batavi was the appointed rendezvous, its excellent harbourage making it convenient both for embarking troops and launching an expedition. For the

Ehine, in one uninterrupted channel, or skirting some islets, branches off", where the Batavian territory commences, as it were, into two streams, one washing the German bank, and preserving its name and its impetuous torrent, till it joins the ocean; the other on the Gallic bank, presenting a wider and smoother surface, the name of which

Wahai. is changed into Vahalis by those dwelling on its shore, a name, however, it soon merges in that

Meuse. of Mosa, from the vast embouchure of which river it also is discharged into the ocean.

7. Meanwhile Csesar, during the passage of the *sums sent* fleet, put Silius in command of a flying corps with *fly- mg corps* orders to make a raid upon the Chatti. He went X«f in person at the head of six legions to a fort on *Ger- mani cus with* the banks of the Lupia, which he had heard was *six legions* of the ships of the Dutch Arctic explorers. 'Built up like a tower both at stem and stern, and presenting in its broad bulbous prow, its width of beam in propor-

tion to its length, its depression amidships.' beleaguered. Nothing was effected by Silius, *secure the* owing to a sudden fall of rain, except the capture " of an inconsiderable booty, with the wife and fj daughter of Arpus, chief of the Chatti. Nor did *f,* the besieging force offer battle to Ceesar, but melted away at the rumour of his approach.

They had, however, pulled to pieces the mound lately erected over the army of Varus, and the old altar of Drusus. The prince restored the altar, and, out of respect to his father, himself at the head of his legions solemnly made its circuit. The mound he did not think it well to rebuild.

All the district also between Fort Aliso and the

Bhine was secured by fortified lines and redoubts.

8. By this time the fleet was come. So send-*Through* ing the commissariat ahead, and assigning ships to Joiningthe our troops and the auxiliaries, he entered the Yssei! canal which bears the name of Drusus, and in-*he,conducts* voking his father, this same Drusus, to aid him *mmLa,* freely and favourably in his adventure on the %, same path, by the pattern and precedent of his *TM* skill as a strategist and engineer, he set off, and had *to the* a prosperous voyage through the lakes and the *ending* sea to the river Amisia. The fleet was left on the *chZusl* left bank of the river, and there was an oversight *ƒ ƒ the Afign* in his not carrying the troops higher up, as their *varu* m march lay through the territory on the right.

The consequence was, that several days were wasted in constructing bridges. And, in fact, the cavalry and regular infantry crossed boldly over the nearest estuary when the tide was out, though the rearmost column of auxiliaries and the Batavians forming part of that body, while displaying

their contempt for the water, and their proficiency as swimmers, were carried away, and some of them drowned. Caesar, while laying out his camp, received intelligence of a revolt of the Angrivarii in the rear, and sent off at once the cavalry and light infantry under Stertinius, who chastised their faithlessness with fire and sword. 9. Between the Eomans and Cherusci ran the *Fiavusand* Visurgis. On its banks stood Arminius, with the *ZIT* rest of the chiefs; and when he had asked whether *£ Weser.*

Caesar was there, and had been told he was, craved leave to speak with his brother. The latter, whose name was Flavus, was a soldier in our army. His loyalty was stainless, and he had lost an eye a few years previously while serving under Tiberius. On permission being given, he stepped out, and was greeted by Arminius, who, dismissing his retinue, demanded the withdrawal of the archers arrayed on our bank; and directly they were gone, asked his brother how his face had got that disfigurement. On the other's stating the place and battle, he eagerly inquired what possible recompense he could have received. Flavus enumerated increase of pay, a collar, a crown, and other military distinctions which Arminius laughed to scorn as the despicable wages of a slave.

10. Forthwith they launched out in opposite strains, Flavus enlarging on the might of Eome, the power of Caesar, the terrible chastisement in store for the vanquished, the pardon held out to voluntary submission, and the anything but unfriendly treatment shown to Arminius's wife and eon; Arminius, on the sanctity of their father *They almost come to blows.* land, their hereditary freedom, the gods of the German hearths, the participation of their mother in his entreaties that Flavus would not elect to be a renegade and traitor to his own kith and kin, aye! and his own nation, rather than be its chieftain. Insensibly they glided into recriminations, and not even the barrier of the river would have prevented their coming to blows, had not Stertinius run up and restrained Flavus, who was foaming with fury, and shouting for his arms and horse. On the opposite side Arminius was to be seen, all threats and menaces of battle. For through most of the dialogue he used the Latin language, which he had learnt when serving as leader of his countrymen in the Eoman army. 11. Next day the German army appeared in *Germani*battle array on the other side of the Visurgis. X *mler.* Ccesar thinking it would be bad generalship to?Stf3 expose his troops to danger before the bridges *skirmish.* and redoubts were complete, threw the cavalry across where the water was fordable. They were led by Stertinius and iEmilius, one of the frontrank men, who crossed at different points so as to distract the enemy. Chariovalda, the Batavian chief, dashed through where the stream ran fastest, and the Cherusci by feigning flight inveigled him into a level space opening out of a fringe of forest-passes, then started up, and pouring upon them at all points, bore down those who resisted, pressed hard on those who gave way, and, when they closed up into a ring, crushed them by simultaneous assaults from a distance and hand to hand. Chariovalda, after long bearing up against the fury of the foe, cheered on his men to break through the swarming masses in a compact body, and while in the act of charging in person through the thickest of the throng, went down under a storm of javelins, with his horse shot under him and many of his chieftains falling round him in a ring. The rest were rescued from their danger either by their own prowess or by the cavalry which Stertinius and iEinilius brought to their help.

12. Caesar, after crossing the Visurgis, was in-*Germani*formed by a deserter that Arminius had selected *ThatZa* battle-field, that other tribes also had gathered " Near to the forest sacred to Hercules, and that they *battlefield.* would venture on a night-attack on the Camp, *pares to* The intelligence was credited. Besides, some '*nhieri* fires were in sight, and the scouts creeping closer reported that they could hear the snorting of steeds and the hum of a mighty and tumultuous host of men. As, therefore, it was clear they were on the eve of a decisive battle, Germanicus thinking it well to sound the disposition of his soldiers, meditated how he could best get at the unvarnished truth. For the reports of tribunes and centurions were too often more agreeable than accurate; freedmen were in spirit still slaves;

friends were apt to flatter. Should he summon an assembly, even there the general acclamation would be the mere echo of the voices of a few.

He must probe their sentiments to the bottom when they were left to themselves, and, free from restraint, gave utterance at their messes to their confidence or misgivings.

13. At the beginning of the night, leaving the *Be mens* divining-quarter secretly and unseen by the sen-*wk%mt* tinels, with only one companion, and wrapped in *Mm.* the skin of a wild beast, he made his way to *fuackty* the camp-streets, stood close to the tents, and gratified himself with the common talk as to his merits; one sounding the praises of his high birth, another of his personal beauty, the majority of his lenience, his affability, his invariable selfpossession in matters grave or gay; vowing that they must show their gratitude on the field of battle, and, to do so, immolate to their revenge and their renown those perjured violaters of the peace. At that moment one of the enemy, acquainted with the Latin language, spurred his horse up to the lines, and in the name of Arminius promised aloud to anyone who should desert, wives and lands and daily pay at the rate of 100 16. *sd.* sesterces per man. At this insult the indignation of the army blazed high. 'Oh for the dawn and the onset! As soldiers, they pledged themselves to take from the Germans their lands, and carry off their wives. They welcomed the presage, and part of the pillage should assuredly be the women, and the treasure of the foe.' About twelve o'clock an assault was made on the camp, but on finding cohorts in force before the fortifications, and no point left unguarded, they retired without discharging a missile. 14. On the same night Germanicus had a happy *Germani*dream. He thought that he was sacrificing, and *lm. He* that the blood of the victims had spirted over *harangues his soldiers,* his robe, whereupon his grandmother Augusta gave him another

and richer one with her own hands. Eeassured by the presage and by favourable omens, he convened an assembly and detailed

the considerations which his experience suggested as adapted to the impending battle. 'Eoman soldiers were by no means efficient only when fighting on open ground, but equally so in woods and forest-passes, if discretion were used. For neither the huge shields of the barbarians nor their monstrous spears could be wielded as easily among the trunks of trees and low brushwood as pila and swords and close-fitting armour. Their blows must be incessant, and they must strike straight at the face. The Germans had neither corselets nor helmets, nor even shields strengthened with iron or thongs, but mere wickerwork or thin pieces of stained wood. The first line, at most, had spears, the rest weapons hardened with fire or of no length. Then their frames, though terrible to the eye and formidable for a sudden onset, were incapable of bearing up under wounds; they would be certain to fly, impenetrable to shame, and deaf to the voice of their leader; recreants in misfortune, they scorned the laws of Heaven and humanity in success. If the soldiers were weary of marches and voyages, and longed for their termination, this was the battle to ensure it; the Elbe was now nearer than the Ehine, and there their warfare would end if they would only help him to leave off as conqueror on the ground that had been the scene of the conquests of the father and uncle in whose footsteps he trod.'

15. Their General's speech roused the enthu-*Harangue* siasm of the soldiers, and the signal for battle was given. On the other side Arminius and the rest of the German chiefs were not remiss in severally reminding their clansmen that 'these Romans were the first in Varus's army to take to their heels, and had turned mutineers to shirk fighting; that, with either their backs a massf of wounds or with limbs battered by wind and wave, without one gleam of hope, they were flying in the face of a foe once more in arms against them and of angry

Heaven. 'Twas plain why they had resorted to ships and the trackless ocean—to avoid opposition to their ingress and being harassed in their retreat. But when once they met hand to hand,

vainly would the vanquished rely on sails and oars. They should think on their enemy's cupidity, ruthlessness, and arrogance, and then what other alternative had they than to maintain their freedom or die ere they were enslaved?'

16. Stimulated by such appeals, and eager for *Description* fray, they were led down into a plain called *stavi*N Idistavisus, which pursues an irregularly winding " .,' aamein. between the Visurgis and the hills, de pending upon the curves of the river or the *troops*.

encroachment of the spurs from the bluffs. In the rear rose a wood with the branches towering aloft and the underground between the boles of the trees quite clear. The plain and outskirts of the wood were occupied by the barbarians, the

Cherusci, by themselves, holding the ridges, so as to pour down on the Eomans in the engagement.

Our men advanced in the following order:—The contingent of Gauls and Germans in the van, fol-

'The first to take to their heels,' etc. Cf. Richard's address to his soldiers, in Beaumont's ' Bosworth Field ':—

'Be still yourselves! ye fight against the dross

Of those who oft have run from you with loss.'

t 'Backs a mass of wounds.' Cf. Ben Jonson's 'Sejanus': —

'Backward ensigns of a slave.'

lowed by the foot-archers; next four legions, and

Caesar at the head of two cohorts of the Praetorians and a picked troop of horse. After them four more legions and the light infantry, with the mounted archers and the remaining auxiliary cohorts. The men were all alert, and ready in a moment to convert the column of march into order of battle.

17. As soon as Caesar caught sight of the *A/amur f-* i i i i . i-i *able omen.*

Uheruscan masses, which had impetuously pressed *Germani*on in front, he ordered the best of the cavalry to a take them in flank, Stertinius, with the remaining *tf _ Germans.* squadrons, to gallop round and fall on them in *Arminius* the rear, promising to support them in person at *guiomerus* the proper moment. And now a most happy ' omen occurred. Eight eagles were seen to fly for and into the wood, and caught the Commander's eye. 'Forwards,' he cries, 'where the eagles of Rome, the guardian powers of the army, lead the way!' As he spoke the infantry advanced, and the cavalry sent ahead burst upon the flanks and rear. And, strange to say, as two columns of the enemy fled in opposite directions, those that had manned the wood plunged into the open flat, and those who had held the plain into the wood. The central force of the Cherusci was now being dislodged. Foremost among them, Arminius, waving and cheering them on and bleeding, maintained the fight. And he had pressed hard upon the The archers, and would have broken through them, Tyrol' had not some cohorts of the Eaetians, Vindelicians, Bavaria. 1 Gauls thrown themselves in the way. As it was, by his personal vigour and the speed of his horse, he made his way through, after smearing his face with his own blood to escape detection. Some have said that he was recognised and let escape by the Chauci serving in the Eoman contingents. Inguiomerus also got away, either by bravery or similar connivance. The rest were cut to pieces indiscriminately. Many, in trying to swim across the Visurgis, were overwhelmed either by a shower of javelins or the current of the stream, and at last by the crush of fugitives and subsidence of the banks. Some caitiff fugitives, who had scrambled to the tree-tops and were cowering behind the boughs, provided excellent sport when the archers were brought up. Others were dashed to pieces by felling the trees.

18. A signal victory this, and one that cost us *Tiberius* small loss. From nine o'clock in the morning till *perator on* nightfall the slaughter of the enemy went on, and *Jphy* for ten miles the

ground was strewn with corpses and weapons, and among the plunder were found chains which, in their certainty of success, they had brought for the Bomans. The soldiers hailed Tiberius Imperator on the battle-field, and threw up a mound on which they piled weapons by way of trophies, with the names of the vanquished nations engraved below. 19. Not all their wounds and woes and losses *This m*roused the Germans to such indignation and fury *Ceriums,* as that spectacle. Those who were just on the *Afresh* point of abandoning their settlements and retiring *position.* Some caitiff.' 'Others climbed the huge walnut-trees that lined the road, seeking concealment in the foliage. A cry of "Crows!" was immediately raised, and the arquebusiers, gathering in a circle, picked them off one by one, while calling to them to spread their pinions, ' etc. 'Battle of Morat,' Kirk's ' Charles The Bold.' or Aller across the Elbe burned for battle and flew to arms. High and low, young and old, they dashed suddenly at the Eonian column and threw it into disorder, and finally took up a position in a small The Leine and marshy flat environed by the river and forest. The forest again was encompassed by a bottomless bog on all sides except one, where the Angrivarii had raised a wide earthwork to mark off their frontier from that of the Cherusci. Here the infantry took their stand. The cavalry lay in the adjacent woods, to take the legions in the rear as soon as they had entered the forest. 20. Nothing of this escaped Caesar. Their plans, *Another* their positions, their overt and covert preparations *mani*were all detected by him, and he proceeded to *'f9TM*turn the enemy's craft to their own confusion. He placed his officer Seius Tubero in charge of the cavalry and the plain. He formed the infantry so as to admit of half entering the forest by the level ground, half storming the earthwork in the way; and this, as being more difficult, he took upon himself, leaving the rest to his officers. Those to whose lot the flat ground had fallen forced their way easily enough. Those who had to carry the earthwork were battered by a storm of blows from above, just as if they were scaling a wall, and the General, seeing they were getting the worst of it at close quarters drew off the legions a little distance and ordered the slingers and engineers to fire a volley and break the ranks of the foe. The catapults came into play; and the defenders, riddled with wounds in consequence of their exposed position, were dislodged. Caesar, at the head of the cohorts of Praetorians, forced the lines and led a charge into the forest, where a fight began hand to hand. The enemy were hemmed in on the rear by a morass, the Eomans by the river or the hills. Both were brought to bay by their position; valour their sole reliance, victory their sole salvation. 21. The Germans were equally brave, but our *Awkward* mode of fighting and our weapons placed them at *%TMmaJl* a disadvantage, the density of their numbers pre-*1TM'TM* venting the full stretch or recovery of their im-*ff*mense spears and the play of their lithe and supple *gives no* forms, now they were brought to close quarters; , while our men, with their shields held tight to their breasts, and their hands gripping the hilts of their swords, lunged at the barbarians' brawny limbs and defenceless faces, striking down a foe at every step. Arminius also had become less alert, either from incessant exposure or because he was crippled by his recent wound. As for Inguiomerus, he showed himself at all points along the line—though unfortunate, unflinching. Germanicus too, in order to facilitate recognition, had taken off his helmet and cheered them on to the slaughter; 'for prisoners were useless, and only the extermination of the nation would be the conclusion of the war.' And now, as the day was far spent, he drew off one legion to form a camp. The rest were glutted with the blood of the enemy till night. The cavalry engagement was indecisive. 22. After publicly complimenting his victorious *Be rakes* army, Cassar heaped up a pile of weapons, with this £ proud inscription:—' The army of Tiberius Cassar, ? »; having subjugated all the tribes between the Ehine *send in* and the Elbe, dedicated this memorial to Mars *their sub*and Jupiter and Augustus.' He added not a word about himself, either from dread of incurring jealousy or satisfied with his own self-approbation. Soon afterwards he sent Stertinius to attack the Angrivarii, who, however, anticipated him by laying down their arms, and, on humbly tendering unqualified submission, were granted a full pardon. 23. But now, as the summer was far advanced, *Part of the* some of the legions were sent back overland to *back over*winter quarters. The major part Cassar put aboard "g ship, and brought to the sea by the river Amisia. *TM ' o J re-embarks* At first the surface was unruffled, save by the *J* throb of a thousand oars or the wake of the ships *Ems to the* under sail. Ere long the hail beat down from the black cloudrack, while the war of waves, as the shifting squalls chopped round to all quarters, shut out all the view and balked their seamanship. And the soldiers, panic-stricken and inexperienced in the perils of the deep, as they got in the way of the sailors or offered them awkward assistance, frustrated the efforts of experience. Anon a hurricane set in from the south, which swept all the heaven and the ocean. Gathering strength in the hilly regions of Germany and the deep rivers and illimitable expanse of clouds, and all the more biting from its vicinity to the bleak North, it drove the vessels hither and thither to the open sea or upon islands bristling with precipitous rocks or hidden shoals. When barely and with much difficulty they had steered clear of these, the tide began to turn and flow with the wind, so that they could neither hold by their anchors nor bale out the seas that broke over them. Horses, beasts of burden, baggage, and even their arms, were tossed overboard to lighten the holds of the weight of water streaming in through leaks and washing over the sides.

24. As the Ocean is stormier than all other *Wrecks* seas, and the climate of Germany is the most *fossTM* tempestuous in the world, so was this disaster of *aemL*an unparalleled and tremendous nature; the sur--. *fTM*

I *palhalory* rounding coasts being unfriendly, or, from its *measures.* seeming, owing to its extent and depth, an illimitThe North able and shoreless sea. Some of the vessels were " swallowed up; a greater number were wrecked Oreades? islands some distance off, and as they were iaies? barren and uninhabited, the soldiers, except such or off as were kept alive on the carcases of horses also and Jut-cast ashore there, were starved to death. Only land Gerinanicus's trireme reached the mainland in the territory of the Chauci; and day and night, upon those shores and promontories, he never ceased to curse himself as the cause of such terrible havoc, and could scarcely be hindered by his friends from making that sea his own grave. At last, as the swell went down and a fair breeze blew, the crippled ships, with an oar or two, or clothes hoisted as sails, and some of them in tow of the less disabled, reassembled, and, after being hastily refitted, were sent off to search the islands. By this forethought, a considerable number were picked up; many also were bought out of the inland districts, and restored by the Angrivarii, who had been lately admitted to our alliance. Some were driven to Britain, and were sent back by the chieftains. In proportion to the remoteness of the regions whence they respectively had returned, they were full of tales of tremendous hurricanes, and fabulous birds, monsters of the

Walruses? deep, strange shapes half human and half beast,
either actually observed or conjured up by terror.
25. The news of the wreck of the fleet at once The news made the Germans hopeful of the issue of the war, "amans. and Cassar eager to keep them down. He ordered ZstlL Caius Silius, with 30,000 infantry and 3,000 *chatti.* cavalry, to march against the Chatti. He in per-*cus chas*

Munster son, with a larger force, burst upon the Marsi, *Marsi.* born their leader Mallovendus, whose submission had recently been accepted, informing him that, buried in a neighbouring wood, there was an eagle of Varus's army kept weakly guarded. Forthwith he despatched a detachment to effect a diversion of the enemy in front, while another party, making a detour to the rear, turned up the soil; both of which enterprises were favoured with success. Inspirited by this, Cassar marched into the interior, scattering desolation and destruction among the foe, who either did not venture on an engagement or were instantly routed wherever they made a stand; and, according to the reports of prisoners, were never more utterly cowed. 'For,' as they declared, 'these Eomans were indomitable, rising triumphant over all misfortunes. Their fleet had been wrecked, their arms lost, the coast was strewn with the carcases of their horses and the corpses of their men, but they had burst on them as fearlessly and fiercely as ever, and apparently in augmented numbers.' 'Strange shapes.' Cf. Motley's 'United Netherlands,' iii. 657:—

'Monsters as large as oxen with almost human faces.' 26. After this, the army was led back to winter-*menus* quarters, full of exultation at having counter-*Germani*balanced their disasters at sea by the success of *Jf,.* their foray. This was crowned by Caesar's gene-*mother .. . n i i y* rosity in indemnifying everyone for his estimated *mand, but* losses. It was, moreover, considered certain that *presses* the enemy were wavering and mooting proposals *timsand* to sue for peace, and that, if he were allowed but this one summer coming, the war might be brought *the comui*to an end. But, in letter after letter, Tiberius urged him to come home for the triumph awarded him. 'He had had adventures enough and hazards enough already; he had fought and won great battles; he should not, however, forget the grievous and cruel losses inflicted by wind and wave, though the general was not to blame. He himself had been sent to Germany by the Immortal Augustus nine times, and had effected more by policy than by the sword. By such means was the adhesion Between of the Sygambri secured; by such means were the ind the Suevi and Maroboduus their king put under the Labn. restraints of peace. The Cherusci and the rest of the insurgent tribes might, now that the honours of Borne had been avenged, be left to their intestine dissensions.' On Germanicus begging for a year to complete his conquests, Tiberius offered a still more tempting bait to his vanity by promising him a second consulship, the duties of which would necessitate his personal attendance; with the additional suggestion that, if there must be more fighting, he should let his brother Drusus have a chance of glory, since he could earn the title of Imperator and win his laurels only in Germany, where only he could find a foe. Germanicus

H hesitated no longer, though he saw through the hypocrisy of it all and the jealousy which snatched him away from reaping a ripe harvest of renown.
27. About the same time, information was laid *uhoprosc*against Libo Drusus, of the family of the Scribonii, "*trnJTM* that he was stirring up a revolution. The progress of this affair I will minutely detail from first to ⱱlast, because discovery was then made, for the first time, of what for many a year gnawed at the vitals of the Commonwealth. Libo, who was young, thoughtless, and easily imposed on, had an intimate friend, named Firmius Catus, a senator, who induced him to resort to predictions of Chaldees, mummeries of magicians, and readers of dreams, by perpetually impressing on him that he was great-grandson of Pompeius, nephew of Scribonia, who had been Augustus's wife, cousin of the Caesars, and of a house rich in ancestral statues; and egged him on to extravagance and debt, participating in his dissipations and liabilities, in order to entangle him in a stronger chain of evidence. 28. When he found that his array of witnesses *Tiberius* (besides some slaves who were privy to the same % facts) was complete, he craved an audience of the 'Jt' *Informer*

Prince, denouncing the crime and the criminal " through the medium of Flaccus Vescularius, a Eoman knight, who was on more intimate terms with Tiberius than himself. Caesar, though he did not disregard the information, refused him an interview, 'for they could continue to exchange communications through the same intermediary.' And in the mean time he promoted Libo to the Praetorship, and entertained him at table, betraying no coldness in his looks, no displeasure in his words, so completely had he masked his resentment. And though he might have put a stop to all Libo's words and acts, he preferred to satisfy his curiosity till one Junius, when Libo had solicited him to conjure up the shades of the dead by incantations, gave information to Fulcinius Trio. Trio's talents were proverbial among the informers, and notoriety was his passion. He pounced on the culprit at once, presented himself before the Consul, and demanded an investigation by the Senate, a meeting of which Tiberius accordingly convened, with special notice that its deliberations were required on a momentous and shocking matter.

29. Meanwhile Libo had put on mourning, and, *Libo in* accompanied by ladies ot rank, was going from *for mercy* house to house, imploring his kinsmen to raise their voices to shield him from danger; in every case meeting with a refusal, under various excuses, though fear was at the bottom of them all. When the Senate met, either broken down by apprehension and anxiety, or, as some have alleged, feigning sickness, he was carried in a litter to the door of the Senate-house, where he leant on his brother, with hand and voice upraised for mercy to Tiberius. But *he* moved not a muscle of his 'A meeting of which.' Augustus had fixed the Calends and Ides of each month as days for the Senate to meet. This was the Senatus Legitimus. Extrordinary meetings were also held, such a meeting being the Senatus Indictus. Four hundred senators had been the number necessary to give any measure force of law. Augustus altered this regulation, arranging by a sort of tariff, that the necessary number should be more or less according to the character of the measure under deliberation. The decision arrived at was, if the necessary number was not present, called senatus auctoritas; if it was, senatus consultum. (Nisard's ' Tacitus.') face at the encounter; and soon afterwards read out the accusations and the accusers' names,

managing to appear neither to extenuate or exaggerate the charge.

30. The other informers, besides Trio and *Tiberius*

Catus, were Fonteius Agrippa and Caius Vibius; *Charges*

and they could not agree which of them should *P*

conduct the case for the prosecution, till Tiberius,

as they could not settle it among themselves, and *of Tiberius*

Libo had come without counsel, undertook to lay *ncTof*

before them the heads of the indictment, and produced papers extravagant in the extreme, such as-He

. again speculations, on Libo's part, whether he would be *pleads for* 360 miles rich enough to pave with gold the Appian Eoad , Braiiisi. f Brundisium, and other things of the same sort, stupid or nighty, or, if you put a more indulgent construction on them, pitiable. The prosecutor leant great stress on some deadly or mysterious characters appended, in one paper, to the names of the Cassars, in Libo's handwriting; and on the prisoner pleading 'Not Guilty,' it was determined to question the slaves by torture; and as, by an old statute of the senate, such question was forbidden in case of a capital charge against a master, the astute Tiberius, an adept at legal innovation, ordered each of them to be sold to the agent of the state, so that depositions against Libo might be extorted from his slaves without infringing the senatorial statute. This made the culprit sue for a trial on the following day; and, going home, he charged his relation, Publius Quirinus, with his last supplications to the Prince. 'Accusations.' Orelli takes libellos to mean the defamatory Writings of Libo. *c* 31. The reply was, 'that he must apply to the *Libo'imi*Senate.' Meanwhile, a guard of soldiers surrounded *banquet.* his house; and already the hubbub they made in the portico forced itself on the eye and ear, when Libo, as he could obtain no respite from his torments, even at the feast he had given as his final revel, began crying for some one to kill him, clutching hold of the slaves' hands and forcing a sword into them. And when they, shrinking back in consternation, upset the lamp standing on a table near them, he, in the darkness of death already closing in on him, wounded himself twice in the vitals. His groans, as he fell, brought up the freedmen in haste, and the soldiers, seeing the work of death, went away. All the formalities, however, of the prosecution were pertinaciously persisted in in the Senate. And Tiberius solemnly declared that, but for this rash suicide, he had intended to intercede for the culprit's life, in spite of his guilt. 32. His property was divided among the in-*Them/or*formers, and extraordinary praelorships conferred on such as were of Senatorial rank. Cotta Messa-*f cy of Mi s* linus then proposed that Livia's bust should not be *saiinus,* carried in the funeral processions oi his descen-*F/occus,* dants; Cneius Lentulus, that no Scribonius should *nius, ml* adopt the surname of Drusus. At the instance of *?PL*Pomponius Flaccus thanksgiving days were de-*nUhmeta* creed. Offerings to Jupiter, Mars, and Concord, *gers. Exe*and the consecration of September 13th, the day *mZnLs.* of Libo's suicide, as a festival, were resolutions of Lucius Piso, Gallus Asinius, Papius Mutilus, and Lucius Apronius. I have recorded the proposals and sycophancy of these men in order to demon Maggiore?

strate the inveteracy of this canker of the State. Enactments of the Senate were also passed for the expulsion of astrologers and magicians from Italy, one of whom, Lucius Pituanius, was hurled from the Tarpeian rock. On another, Publius Marcius, the Consul, inflicted the old-fashioned punishment, Porta by proclamation of trumpet outside the Esquiline Gate. 33. At the next session of the Senate, Quintus *Haterius .. andFronto*

Haterius, ex-consul, and Octavms Pronto, ex-*inveigh*

prastor, inveighed at length against the extravagance of society, and an act was passed against making services of solid gold, and the effeminacy - *precatesin* of men's wearing silken clothes. Fronto went *terfermce.* further, and called for restrictions upon plate, furniture, and slaves. For up to this time it was habitual for the Senators when it came to their turn to speak to the question to put forward any suggestions they might think conducive to the public weal.

In opposition to this, Gallus Assinius urged ' That private property had grown with the growth of the empire, and there was no novelty in this, for it had been the rule time out of mind. A fortune meant one thing to a Fabricius, another thing to a

Scipio, but was in all cases proportionate to the prosperity of the State, for when it was insignificant, its members' households were on a small

'To speak to the question'; i.e., as I understand it, to say,

when it came to their turn, on which side they voted, e.g. 'Die, Porci,' 'Censeo Carthaginem esse delendam.' The senators sat in order. Each voted in order (suo loco sententiam dicere. Cic.)

A senator might, instead of simply voting, give reasons for his vote, that is, digress from a categorical reply to the question, hut not as a rule digress to any other topic. Of. c. 38. But 'loco sentential' seems generally to he taken to mean, '*instead* o/"merely voting.'

scale, and along with its advance to its present splendour, the affluence of individuals kept pace. In the case either of the slaves or plate, and all articles of utility, the only standard of extravagance or moderation was the owner's means. The difference between the assessments of a senator and a knight was not because of any intrinsic distinction between them, but that such appliances as promote peace of mind or bodily health, should belong to them in a measure corresponding to their priority of place, rank, and office; lest haply in proportion to a man's distinction his responsibilities should be more numerous, his risks more heavy, while solace for those risks and responsibilities he

would have none.' The good face put upon admitted failings, together with the sympathy of his audience, procured for Gallus cordial acquiescence. Tiberius, too, had remarked that it was not the time for such supervision, and in case of any deterioration in morals there would be no lack of an initiator of reform.

34. Whereupon Lucius Piso, with an invective *Piso says* against intrigues of the forum, the corruption of *some!!!* the Courts, and the truculence of those speakers who had threats of indictment ever on their hps, *nia. Her* declared that he would go away and withdraw , from the city, and live in some secluded and remote country-spot, quitting the Senate House as he concluded. This stung Tiberius, and besides soft speeches of his own to conciliate Piso, he incited 'Admitted failings ': i.e. the 'confessio vitiorum' contained in Gallus's speech, who, however, veiled it 'sub honestis nominibus.'

Orelli says that the ' confessio ' was the tacit admission of guilt on the part of his audience.

his relatives also to restrain him from taking his departure by their influence or entreaties. This same Piso exhibited a freeman's indignation in an equally marked manner by summoning for trial Urgulania, whom Augusta's friendship had exalted over the law. Urgulania paid no regard to the summons, but to show her contempt for Piso went in her litter to Caisar's house. But he on his side was equally pertinacious in spite of Augusta's complaints of his outrageous insolence to her. Tiberius, thinking that, without giving offence, he might so far gratify his mother as to promise to present himself at the bar of the Praetor, and defend Urgulania, set out to the palace, after telling his body-guard to follow at some distance behind. He was to be seen amid the thronging crowd, looking collected, and protracting the time and the walk by conversation of all sorts, till as his relatives failed to restrain Piso, Augusta ordered the sum demanded to be paid down. And so the matter ended, Piso emerging from it not without credit, and Cajsar with aug-

mented reputation. Urgulania's influence was, notwithstanding, so excessive in Eome that she scorned to appear as witness in a case that was before the Senate. The Praetor was sent to take her depositions in her own house, though by long precedent even the Vestal virgins, when they gave evidence, gave it in open court. 35. I should not mention the interruption of business this year if it were not worth while to S«» notice the conflicting opinions of Cneius Piso and Asinius Gallus about the matter. Piso, though *noadvo*Ccesar had announced his intention to be absent, *Asinius* for that very reason recommended despatch, in *opposes the* order that the ability of the Senate and Knights *fanaftu in* to discharge their functions in the absence of the Prince might redound to the credit of the State. Gallus, as Piso had anticipated him in the ostentation of freedom, said that in his opinion no transaction could be august enough, or worthy of the Eoman people, unless it was in the hearing and under the eye of the Caesar, and therefore that the concourse from Italy and influx of the provincials should be postponed until he was present. This was said in Tiberius's hearing, and as he made no remark, it was hotly debated on both sides. However, they decided on postponement. 36. A dispute also arose between Gallus and *Gallus* Cassar, the former recommending that magis-*uctimt* trates should be elected for five years, and that *ateTfive* officers of legions who had served in that capacity *tt* ITT T 1 111-" previous to holding the prastorship, should m *Tiberius* virtue of it be designated as prastors, and that , the prince should nominate twelve candidates every year. It was plain enough that this proposal had a deeper meaning, and struck at the roots of the Government. Tiberius, however, assuming that it added to his power, urged 'that to make so many selections and inflict so many disappointments was repugnant to his delicacy. 'Elected for five years.' A general of an army, even if he had only been praetor, called himself legatus consularis. An officer of a legion, even though not praetor, called himself legatus praetorius. So that his rank became in a way like that of praetor, and he could become a candidate for the office on his return home. But if magistrates were nominated five years in advance these officers of legions would have their chance postponed for the same time. So Gallus demanded that in right of their military grade they should be praetors-nominate. (Nisard.)

Even with annual elections it was hard to avoid incurring odium, though rejection was less mortifying when another opportunity was so close;

how great then would be the rancour of men who were made to wait more than five years. And how was it possible to foresee, so far ahead, anyone's disposition, domestic circumstances, or estate? How arrogant it made men to be designated a year in advance! What would be the effect if they could speculate on the office for five years?

Practically the term of office would be multiplied fivefold, and those laws rendered null which assigned the proper time for testing the candidate's assiduity, and for the pursuit and possession of office.'

By a speech apparently so public-spirited he retained the reins of Government in his own hands.

37. He also augmented the income of some of *Hortaius* the Senators, which made all the more remarkable *'senate for* his chilling reception of the petition of Marcus *P%* Hortalus, a young man of high birth, whose indigence was notorious. He was the grandson of Hortensius, the orator, and had been induced by the Immortal Augustus, who made him a 8333 6 8 present of a million sesterces, to marry a wife and propagate children, so as to avert the extinction of so illustrious a line. On these grounds, he stationed his four children at the entrance to the Senate, which was then sitting at the palace, and when it came to his turn to speak to the question, with his eyes turned now on the bust of Hortensius ranged amongst the orators, now on that of Augustus, he began to this effect, 'Conscript 'The term of office.' Or 'Magistrate' may mean the 'Magistrates.'

Fathers, I became the father of all these young children whom you see before you not of my own inclination, but at the instigation of the Prince. Not that my ancestors had not been right worthy of descendants. For, as for myself, though I had been debarred from the possession or acquisition of wealth or popularity or eloquence—the hereditary endowment of our family—by the vicissitudes of the times, I was yet satisfied so long as my indigence was neither humiliating to myself, nor burdensome to others. It was at the Sovereign's command that I married. There stand the scions and sons of that long list of consuls and dictators. Not that I remind you of these facts reproachfully, but to enlist your compassion. While fortune smiles on you, Cassar, they will rise to such a position as you may bestow on them. Meanwhile, preserve from penury the great-grandsons of Quintus Hortensius, the foster sons of the Immortal Augustus.' 38. The Senate was disposed to favour Hortalus, *Tiberius,s* which was quite sufficient to move Tiberius to offer more energetic opposition in a speech almost

D *rl* jr *7i axes pro word* for word as follows: 'If once a precedent is *vmonfor* given for all who are paupers to come here and demand charity for their children, individuals will never be satisfied, and the state will become bankrupt. It is a privilege we have derived from our forefathers to make an occasional digression from the question, and, on the turn for our opinion coming, to propound what we think may tend to the public weal; but it was assuredly never contemplated that we should subserve here our private interests and domestic circumstances, and subject the Senate and Prince to equal disparagement whether they happened to have accorded or refused a grant. And in this case it is not solicitation but importunity, importunity, too, ill-timed and without fair notice, to rise up in a meeting of the Senators for other business, and pleading the number and youth of a family to trespass on the Senate's delicacy; then bring the same pressure to bear on me, and, so to speak, take the treasury by

storm; for if we allow it to be drained by mendicity it must be replenished by crime. The Immortal Augustus did, Hortalus, it is true, give you money, but without solicitation or any stipulation that it should be a permanent grant. Else industry will be disheartened, and an incentive given to indolence, if each intrinsically presents no stimulus to hope or fear. Everyone will tranquilly rely upon the alms of other persons, and useless to themselves be a drag upon us.' This and similar language, though listened to with acquiescence by those who habitually eulogise all that comes from Princes, whether good or bad, was received by the majority in silence, or with a stifled groan. And Tiberius noticing this, said, after a short pause, 'That his answer was given to Hortalus; if, however, the Senate approved, he would 1666 18 4 give to each of the male children 200 sestertia.' All except Hortalus expressed their gratitude. He said not a word, either out of trepidation, or because in his distressed circumstances he still clung to his hereditary pride. And after this Tiberius never showed him any pity, though the Hortensian house sank into shameful indigence.

39. The same year the daring of a single slave *A slave of* would, but for timely prevention, have convulsed *ripp . .. Postumua* the state with dissension and civil war. His name *coiled cu* was Clemens, and he belonged to Postumus 'JTa Agrippa, and, on hearing of Augustus's death, in anything but the spirit of a slave, he formed the *EtmtmPianosa.* idea of sailing to the island of Planasia, carrying off Agrippa by force or fraud, and bringing him to the armies in Germany. The slowness of a merchant vessel thwarted his plans, and as in the meantime Agrippa had been killed he launched out into a wider and more desperate scheme, and Monte stealing Agrippa's ashes sailed to Cosa, a promonArgentaro. . f truria, where he hid himself in desolate spots till his hair and his beard were grown. For in age and appearance he was not unlike his master. Then he set a rumour afloat by telling agents and accomplices that

Agrippa was still alive. At first, as is usually the case with forbidden topics, it took the shape of mysterious intimations which by and by circulated everywhere among the ignorant and credulous who eagerly drank them in, and also among seditious people anxious for a revolution. He himself began to visit the towns in the evening, never showing himself openly or for any length of time at the same place. But knowing that truth gains by leisurely investigation, imposture by precipitancy and mystery, he always left a place where he was becoming too much talked of to *He comes to* present himself where he was unknown. *Ostiaand* r *is entrap* 40. Meanwhile, the rumour that Agrippa had been saved by the goodness of Heaven grew rife 'He always,' etc. Or, 'he always withdrew betimes from publicity or forestalled it.' through Italy, and was gaining credit at Rome, *ped by* Already the impostor was welcomed by a vast *fakm'be*throng at Ostia, and by secret meetings at Eome; while Tiberius was perplexed by anxious uncer- tainty whether he should crush this slave of his *cuted.* by armed force or leave the delusion to be dispelled merely by time. Wavering between shame and apprehension he reasoned one moment that nothing was too slight to be disregarded, the next, that everything ought not to excite his alarm; in the end, ordering Sallustius Crispus to take the matter in hand. He chose two of his dependents, who some say were soldiers, and instructed them to get access to Clemens, profess complicity, be liberal with their money, and swear to render him faithful and unflinching service. They executed their orders, and one night when they found him off his guard procured an adequate force and dragged him off to the Palace, bound and gagged. They say that when Tiberius inquired 'how he had transformed himself into Agrippa,' he retorted, 'as you transformed yourself into a Caesar.' Nothing could compel him to betray his accomplices; and Tiberius, as he dared not execute him publicly, ordered him to be put to death in a secluded part of the palace, and the corpse to be privately carried away.

And though many of the Prince's household, both of equestrian and senatorial rank, were said to have supported him with their purses and aided him by their advice, no investigation ensued. 41. At the end of the year dedication was *consecra*made of an arch near the Temple of Saturn, to £££ commemorate the recovery of the standard lost *TMm 'cuss tri* under Varus, recovered under the leadership of «««»».
Germanicus and Tiberius's happy star; of a temple *Forelo*to Fors Fortuna, in the gardens near the Tiber, *people.,* left by the dictator Ctesar to the people of Home; and of a chapel to the Julian family, and a statue to the Immortal Augustus, near Fratocdii. Bovhieb. In the consulships of Caius Caslius and Lucius Pomponius, on May 25, Germanicus Cassar celebrated a triumph over the Cherusci, Chatti, and Angrivarii, and all the other nations as far as the Elbe. In the procession were the spoils and the prisoners, and representations of mountains and battles; and since only his orders had hindered him concluding the war, they assumed that it was concluded. His extreme personal beauty and the car which bore his five sons, heightened the admiration of the spectators, but there was an under-current of dread latent in their minds as they remembered how fatal had been the prepossession of the populace to his father Drusus; Cf. En. how also his uncle Marcellus had been snatched - away in the flower of his youth from the passionate attachment of the lower order; how short-lived and ill-starred were the favourites of the Eoman people.
£2 io. 42. Tiberius, on his part, gave three hundred *Largess of* sesterces a man to the lower order in the name of 5) Germanicus, and nominated himself as his col-*?pvf 'eta. Ar* league in the consulship. But, as he acquired *cheiam,* none the more credit for disinterested affection, *whom Tibe*he determined to get the young man out of the *JgT,"* way on pretence of promoting him, and devised "XmT an opportunity or clutched at one which chance ? *dies. Cap* afforded. For fifty years Archelaus had been *padotia* King of Cappadocia, and was

detested by Tiberius, *province,* because he had paid him no attentions during his *and the one* stay at Ehodes. Not that it was pride that made f,"'" Archelaus negligent, but warnings he had received " from intimate acquaintances of Augustus, since as *Deaths of* Caius Caesar's fortunes were so prosperous, and *of Commahe* had been sent on a mission to the East, it was *phUopator* considered hazardous to befriend Tiberius. When £ . *lyyria ana,* the latter obtained the sovereignty through the *Judaa* extinction of the race of the Caesars, he entrapped *of taxa*Archelaus by means of a letter from his mother, " in which, without concealing her son's repugnance, she still held out hopes of mercy if he would come in person to ask it. Archelaus, unsuspicious of fraud, or fearing force if he should be supposed to see through it, hurried to Eome where the Prince gave him a stern reception; and he was before long arraigned before the Senate. And, though it was not owing to such mendacious charges, yet partly from vexation, partly also from the feebleness of age, and because kings, who brook no equals, can least bear degradation, he died either a natural death or by his own hand. The kingdom was reduced to a province, and Caesar, declaring that its produce would warrant an abatement of the one per cent, tax, fixed it for the future at half that amount. About the same time the deaths of Antiochus, King of Commagene, and Philopator, King of Cilicia, threw their dominions into commotion, as some were for regal government, while the majority desired that of Eome. Also the provinces of Syria and Judaea, groaning under their imposts, entreated for a reduction of the tax. 43. Tiberius, therefore, urged these subjects on *Extraordi*the Senate, and also the state of Armenia as pre-*nary* viously recorded, together with the impossibility *tUEa&t* of quelling the ferment in the East except by the *J?.* ability of Germanicus, for his own life was on the *"f-f'* , *character.* wane, and Drusus had not yet reached his prime, *whyhewa*
So, by order of the Senate, Germanicus was placed *Syria. Cli* in command of

the provinces beyond the sea, with *slrm-for* and the authority wherever he went superior to those who *S* provinces. *ana trer* in Africa, owed their place to allotment, or were delegates of the Prince. Now Tiberius had withdrawn *manicus. Their union. Contract their wivet.* from Syria Creticus Silanus, between whom and jera
Germanicus there were matrimonial ties, (Silanus's daughter being betrothed to Nero, Germanicus's eldest son,) and had placed over it Cneius Piso.
He was a man of a turbulent and doggedly independent character, in whose veins ran the hot blood of his father—that Piso, who in the civil war gave the most energetic assistance to the fresh rising in Africa against Caesar; then sided with
Brutus and Cassius; and, after he had obtained leave to return to Eome, had refrained from all solicitation for office, till he was prevailed upon to accept a consulship which was none of his own seeking but pressed on him by Augustus. And,
over and above his hereditary imperiousness, he was so puffed up by the high-birth and wealth of his wife Plancina, that he would barely yield precedence to Tiberius, and as for Tiberius's children looked down on them as infinitely his inferiors.
He never questioned but that he had been selected as Governor of Syria, expressly to thwart Germanicus's projects. Some people have supposed
'In whose veins.' Or, who had inherited the imperious spirit.'

I that Tiberius even gave him secret orders, and it is certain that Augusta, as she persecuted Agrippina with all a woman's jealousy, gave Plancina her cue. For suppressed predilections for Drusus or Germanicus split up the court into factions and feuds. Tiberius naturally supported Drusus, his own son, and born of his own blood. As for Germanicus, his uncle's estrangement only increased the enthusiasm of the people for him, coupled as it was with the superior lustre of his lineage on the mother's side. For he could point to Marcus Antonius as his grandfather, Augustus

as his uncle, while the great-grandfather of Drusus was a simple Eoman knight, and seemed unworthy of the place he occupied among the busts of the Claudian House. Agrippina, too, Germanicus's wife, both in the number of her children and in reputation, eclipsed Drusus's wife Livia. With all this, the brothers were singularly united and unaffected by the strife of their relations.
44. Soon after this, Drusus was sent to Illyri-*Drusus* cum to serve his apprenticeship as a soldier, and *thedissT* win the affections of the army, and also because Tiberius reflected that a youth, who was running *iuyncum* riot in the dissipation of the town, would be more *text of* under control in the camp, while he himself would *een'* be more secure when each of his sons was in *auiis and* command of the troops. His pretext, however, *Arminius.* was an application from the Suevi for aid against the Cherusci. For when the Eomans had evacuated their country and they had nothing to fear from foreigners, according to the national habit, and at that time especially from rivalry in renown, they had come to blows among themselves. In strength and the ability of their chiefs, the tribes were well-matched, but his regal title made Maroboduus detested among his countrymen, while they were attached to Arminius as the champion of freedom.
45. Hence not only the Cherusci and their *The Sem.* allies, Arminius's old soldiers, flew to arms, but *Lj!* even of Maroboduus's own subjects, the Semnones ffo West of and Langobardi— clans of the Suevi—went over to *rminius.* the Elbe,,.. ....... *Inguw* near the nis rival. And their accession would nave given *mems u*Chanci. preponderance, if Inguiomerus with a *Maloto* body of dependents had not deserted to Maro- boduus, his only reason being that submission to "3«e' *before* his own nephew and a young man, was what he, *battle.*
as his uncle and in his old age, could not brook.
The armies confronted each other in battle array,
equally confident, and with none of

those desultory onsets and disorderly masses hitherto characteristic of Germans, for, from long warfare against us, they had learnt to keep to their ranks, to strengthen themselves by reserves, and to obey their General's orders. And on this occasion
Arminius inspected the whole army on horseback,
and, as he rode up to each body, reminded the soldiers of the freedom they had regained, of the legions they had cut to pieces, of the plunder and weapons which they had wrested from the Eomans, and bore, many of them, in their hands that day. Then he launched into denunciations of Maroboduus as a dastard who knew not what battle was, who had skulked in the recesses of the
Hercynian forest, and then by deputations and donations sued for terms, who was a traitor to his fatherland and an underling of Caesar, to be extirpated with as little compunction as when they slew Quintilius Varus. Many were the battles— would they only recall them—the issue of which, together with their final expulsion of the Eomans, showed plainly enough who had carried off the honours of the war. 46. Maroboduus also was by no means sparing *Marobo* of self-glorification and vituperation of the foe. *harangue.* But, laying his hand on Inguiomerus, he protested ST that in the man before them was centred all the £ws glory of the Cherusci, and that all that had been
" *appeals for* managed by his advice had turned out well, *aid to .." , . ....* Tiberius.
Arminius was a madman, who, with no experience of his own, appropriated to himself the credit due to another: for what had he done but surprise three negligentf legions, and a general not dreaming of treachery, and with no other result than ruinous loss to Germany and degradation to himself, since his own wife and son were languishing in slavery to that very hour. He, on the other hand, though assailed by twelve legions with Tiberius at their head, had preserved the honour of the Germans untarnished, and after a time retired from the struggle on equal terms; and he by no

means regretted having placed at their own disposal the alternative of making war on Eome with unimpaired vigour or making peace without loss of blood. ' Such were the words which fired the two armies, who had moreover motives of their own to spur them on; since the Cherusci and Langobardi were fighting for old renown or newly-won 'Who had carried off.' Or, 'who had borne the brunt of.' + 'Negligent.' Cf. Sallust, 'J. ,' 52, 6. According to Orelli 'without a leader,' but he does not explain satisfactorily how a leaderless legion could have 'ducem fraudis ignarum.' freedom, and the other side for the extension of their dominion. Never was there a more furious encounter, never one more indecisive in its results. For the right wing in both armies was routed, and a renewal of the battle was expected when Maroboduus drew off his army to the hills. This was a confession of defeat, and, as he was abandoned by his men in successive desertions, he fled to the Marcomanni, and sent an embassy to Tiberius to sue for aid. The reply was that he had no right to call in the forces of Eome against the Cherusci, after having never given the Komans the smallest assistance when they were fighting against the same foe. However, Drusus was sent, as I have stated, to restore peace. A.d. 17. 47. That same year twelve populous cities of *Twelve* Asia were shattered by an earthquake which *Asia* happened during the night, so that the blow was ,, all the more abrupt and appalling. And the usual resource in such a calamity—flight into some *Remedial ...II measures.* open space—was here ot no avail, as the earth yawned and swallowed them up. It is said that lofty mountains were levelled, tracts that had been level reared aloft, and that flames flashed out amid the havoc. As the calamity fell on the people Sart. of Sardis with most severity, their case excited most compassion, Caesar promising them ten mil83,333 6 8 hon sesterces and five years' remission of all dues to the national or imperial exchequer. Next to them the largest amount of suffering and relief fell Manissa. to the Magnesians of Mount Sipylus. The Senate Menimen, determined that the Temnians, Philadelphians, Allah Hisar? j32geatans, Apollonidians, and the people called ' 'Was expected.' Or, 'they were eager for,'

Mostenians and Macedonian Hyrcanians, along Sandariik? with the towns of Hierocaasarea, Myrina, Cyme, Maga and Tmolus should for the same period be exempted Dagh. from their taxes, and that a commissioner should be despatched to examine into their present necessities and relieve them. Marcus Aletius, one of the ex-pra3tors, was selected to prevent the rivalry and consequent inconvenience which might arise if they chose any one of equal rank with the Governor of Asia who was an ex-Consul.

48. Caesar crowned these splendid bounties to *Tiberius, disi/tx tcf* communities by a generosity equally gracious in *ested con*resigning to iEmilius Lepidus the property of *Matter of'* iEmilia Musa, a rich freedwoman, as she was ap-*9 Cases of* parently a member of the same house, though, *Lepidm* since she had died without a will, it was forfeited *Servilius.* to the Imperial treasury. Also, though part of *Amdus,* the estate of Patuleus, a rich Eoman Knight, was *f$%i* devised specially to him, he resigned it to Marcus *expelled* Servilius, because he found Servilius declared heir *Senate.* in a previous and perfectly authentic document.

In both cases, his preliminary remark was that their high rank must not be penniless. Indeed, he would not accept any one's estate, unless ties of friendship gave him some claim to it. From strangers and people who merely from personal pique named the prince their heir, he stood peremptorily aloof. On the other hand, if he relieved respectable people whose penury was owing to no fault of their own, he also expelled from the Senate, or sanctioned the voluntary withdrawal, of those who were spendthrifts and reduced to indigence by depravity, such as Vibidius

Varro, Marius Nepos, Appius Appianus, Cornelius
Sulla, and Quintus Vitellius.

49. About the same time Tiberius consecrated *Comecra-*
some temples which had been consumed by age *Temples.*
or fire, and which Augustus had commenced rebuilding; also one to Liber, Libera, and Ceres,
near the Great Circus, in fulfilment of a vow of R.c. 495. the dictator Aulus Postumius; a shrine to Flora built in the same place by Lucius Publicius and Marcus Publicius when they were asdiles; a temple to Janus which had been erected at the vegetR.c. 259. kl market by Caius Duilius, the first Eoman commander, who won a victory by sea, and earned a naval triumph over the Carthaginians. Germanicus consecrated a shrine to Hope which Aulus Atilius had vowed in the same war.

50. During all this time the Law of Treason *Varilia* was growing more stringent. And Appuleia *treason* Varilia, Augustus's erand-niece, was accused of *f*
'D o' *Augustus,* treason by an informer, because she had spoken in scandalous and disrespectful terms of the Im-*and of* mortal Augustus, Tiberius, and Tiberius's mother; *mJriuS*
and because, though Cassar's relation, she was convicted of adultery. As to her adultery, the provisions of the Julian law seemed to meet her case. In the indictment for treason, Caesar required that the counts should be dealt with separately, and that she should be condemned if she had spoken irreverently of Augustus, but he would not have any notice taken of disparagement of himself. On the Consul's inquiring what was his decision as to the aspersions she was accused of uttering against his mother, he made no reply.

But, afterwards at the next meeting of the Senate,
*moderation.* he begged in his mother's name also that no vituperation of her should be in any way accounted criminal, and acquitted Appuleia of treason. He also procured mitigation of the severest penalty for adultery, recommending that, in accordance with old

precedent, her relatives should remove her two hundred miles from Eome. Her paramour Manlius was banished from Italy and Africa.

51. A strife arose about the election of a Pras-*Germani*tor as a substitute for Vipstanus Gallus, who had *Drusus in* been carried off by death. Germanicus and Drusus, "T*fthe* who were then at Eome, favoured Haterius Agrip-f *P*

'. *Poppaa* pa, Germanicus's kinsman. The majority, on the *support* other hand, insisted on the number of the candi-*candida*dates' children turning the scale, according to *pZtoT-* Lex Papia law. Tiberius was delighted to see the Senate £j%, Popp-adjudicating between his sons and the law. It is true that the law was set aside, but not immediately, and only by a few votes, exactly as laws, when laws had real weight, were set aside.

A..D. 17. 52. The same year a war broke out in Africa, *Tacfarinas* the enemy being headed by Tacfarinas. He was *Africa*.

East by birth a Numidian, but had served among the *and tactTM*.

Algiers. iliaries in the Eoman army, had afterwards deserted, and, first by banding together vagabonds - familiar with brigandage, for pillage and rapine,

whom he then organised in military fashion by squads and squadrons, came at last to be looked on as chieftain, not of an undisciplined gang, but of the Musulamians. This powerful tribe, dwelling

Tunis. on the borders of the desert of Africa, which up to that time possessed no cities, took up arms,

and drew along with them into the war their

Fesszan, neighbours the Moors. The leader of the latter was Mazippa. A division was made of the forces,

on the principle of Tacfarinas keeping in camp the pick of the troops, armed in Eoman fashion, and training them to discipline and obedience, while Mazippa, with the light-armed forces, spread fire and sword and terror far and wide. And they

Part of had coerced the Cinithii, a people of considerable

Tripoli. importance, to join them, when Furius Camillus, Proconsul of Africa, concentrated one legion and all the allies under his command and led them against the enemy. The force was small enough if compared with the numbers of the Numidians and Moors, but his principal apprehension was lest fear should make them shrink from fighting. It was by a prospect of victory that they were lured to defeat. So he posted the legion in the centre, and the light cohorts with two squadrons on the wings. Tacfarinas, for his part, did not decline the battle. The Numidians were routed, 40o. and for the first time for many years the name of Furius acquired military renown. For since the famous restorer of Eome, and Camillus his son, the reputation of generalship had been confined to other branches of the family, and the one whom I have noticed was esteemed but an indifferent soldier. This made Tiberius all the more ready to eulogise his exploits before the Senate, and the

Cf. i. 72. Senators voted him the triumphal distinctions which, owing to his unassuming character, proved uninjurious to him.

53. Next year Tiberius was Consul for the *Germani*third, Germanicus for the second time. But Ger-*voyage to* Prevesa. manicus entered upon that office at Nicopolis, in j& *visit's* Achaia, where he had arrived by route of the coast of Ulyricum from a visit to his brother *Athenian* Drusus, who was then staying in Dalmatia. In *ancy.* the Adriatic, and afterwards the Ionian Sea, he had had a stormy voyage, so that he stayed a few days to refit his fleet, taking the opportunity to Gulf of visit the bay famous for the victory of Actium, ' the spoils dedicated by Augustus, and the camp of Antonius, all of which brought his ancestors to his recollection. For he was, as I have said, great-nephew to Augustus, grandson of Antonius, and the ground brought vividly before his imagination memories both of pleasure and of pain. Thence he went to Athens, and, in deference to a city which was an ally and of such venerable associations, employed only one lictor. The Greeks welcomed him with most elaborate honours, and, in order to enhance the value of their flattery, paraded all that their ancestors had said or done in days of yore.

Negro-54. From Athens he sailed to Eubcea, and crossed *He coasts*

Meteiin. over to Lesbos, where Agrippina gave birth to *Minor, re*Julia, her youngest child. Next he penetrated to *pvinces* Erekii. the far limits of Asia, and to Perinthus and By- nonoffl"' zantium, cities of Thrace; soon afterwards to the *p f P-*' note. His

Sea of Straits of Propontis and the mouth of the Euxine, *death fore*

Marmora. ,,..,,.... *told at* irom curiosity to become acquainted with localities *clans.* so old and so renowned. And as he went he relieved such provinces as were groaning under intestine discord or the oppression of their magistrates. On his return he made an attempt to be Samo-present at the celebration of the Samothracian thrati. *ut* was driven away by northerly headwinds. So, after going over Hium and all that is there venerable from the vicissitudes of its for tunes and from its being the cradle of our race he resumed his voyage along the coast of Asia, and put in at Colophon in order to consult the *zm«?* oracle of Apollo of Claros. There is not a priestess there as at Delphi, but a priest appointed from select families, generally belonging to Miletus, who notices only the number and names of the applicants, then withdraws into the cave, and, after a draught from the water of a secret spring, though most frequently illiterate and destitute of poetic skill, makes answer in lines in unison with the thoughts passing in the applicant's mind. And it was said that darkly, as oracles ever do, he chanted to Germanicus his early doom.

55. Meanwhile Cneius Piso, in order to com-*Piso's 't ,i j i i i roughness* mence his mission the sooner, made his entry into *the* Athens in a rough way, which struck terror into *jTM* its inhabitants, and then abused them in a savage *. has a* speech with a covert attack on Germanicus for *grudge*. having degraded the

majesty of Eome by treating *fte7and* with extravagant respect people who, instead of being the Athenians, who had been annihilated *TM??* . '... *Bhodes.* by a long series of calamities, were the offscouring *Germani*of the world. As for Athens, she had been the *ttmfZm* ally of Mithridates against Sulla, of Antonius against the Immortal Augustus. He even cast in their *T$:* , *Plancina s* teeth events of old times—their impotent efforts *un/eminine* against the Macedonians and their outrages on their own citizens— being embittered by personal pique against the city for not having pardoned, on his entreaty, a man of the name of Theophilus, who had been convicted of fraud by the Areopagus. 'In lines in unison.' Or compositis may mean 'polished.' Cf. i. 1.

From Athens he made all sail through the Cyclades and the shortest sea passage, and off Ehodes overtook Germanicus, who was well aware of the spitefulness with which he had been assailed. Nevertheless he displayed such remarkable generosity that when a storm sprang up and drove his enemy upon reefs, and his death would have been attributed to accident, he sent triremes, by help of which Piso was rescued from danger. The other, however, was not at all melted, and chafing even at a day's delay, he parted company with Germanicus and got ahead of him. And directly he reached the army in Syria, by gifts, by intrigues, by bounties to the humblest privates, by displacing the old centurions and strict tribunes and appointing to their posts creatures of his own or all the worst characters, by permitting the men to be idle in camp, to commit excesses in the towns, to run riot in the country, he was so successful in tampering with them that in the mouths of the common soldiers he was known as the 'father of the army.' Even Plancina must needs transgress feminine decency and attend at manoeuvres of cavalry and evolutions of cohorts, and scatter broadcast insults against Agrippina and Germanicus. And even some of the better disposed sol 'By gifts, by intrigues,' ete. Cf. 'The Tempest/ Act I., Sc. H.

Thy false uncle
Being once perfected how to grant suits,
How to deny them; whom to advance, and whom
To trash for overtopping; new created
The creatures that were mine, I say, or changed them,
Or else new form'd them; having both the key
Of officer and office, set all hearts i' the state
To what tune pleased his ear.' ,

diers were ready to show a base subservience,
because there was a whispered, report prevalent that all this was not displeasing to the Imperator.
Germanicus was aware of what was going on,
but he was above all things anxious to reach
Armenia.

56. Armenia from of old has been an unsettled *Germani*nation, owing both to the nature of its people and its "*zLTm the* geographical position; for it forms a large frontier *fTMTM* to our province and yet stretches all the way to *Cdfypci* Media; and is always on bad terms with the *dctia into* powerful nations on either side of it, opposing the *tndvZ*Eomans as foes, the Parthians as rivals. At that time it had no king. Vonones had been deposed. But popular inclination leaned towards Zeno, son *gene.* of Polemo, King of Pontus. For he, by affecting from his earliest boyhood the customs and manners of the Armenians—at the hunt, and the banquet, and all the other usages of barbarians—had won the attachment both of high and low. Therefore Germanicus, with the approval of the chiefs, and surrounded by a throng of people, placed on his brow the symbol of royalty in the city of Nakhit-Artaxata. Everyone else bowed the knee, hailing chevan. hi ag Bang Artaxias, a word they had framed from the name of the town. Cappadocia was reduced to a province, and Quintus Veranius deputed its governor. Some abatement of the royal tribute was made, to inspire hope of the relative lenience of the Eoman rule. Quintus Servasus was put in charge of Commagene, which was then for the first time transferred to the jurisdiction of a prastor.

57. But Germanicus was deprived of his satis-*Piso's con*faction at this successful settlement of the affairs *tumacious*of the allies by the insolence of Piso, who had *meets Git*received orders to lead in person, or send by his son, some of the legions to Armenia, and had *Theypart open joes.*
Kars. omitted to do either. At last they met at Cyrrhus, *His in*where were the winter-quarters of the tenth legion, *banquet.* each forcing up a show of composure—Piso lest he should seem afraid, and Germanicus to avoid the semblance of intimidation; and he really was, as I have mentioned, of an indulgent disposition. But his friends, by craftily inflaming grievances, exaggerated what was true and fabricated lies, and brought specific accusations against Piso, Plancina, and their sons. At length, in the presence of only a few friends, Caesar began to speak in language such as resentment and the attempt to hide it dictates, Piso replying with ironical humility. And they parted open foes. From that time Piso seldom took his seat by Caesar on the judgment-bench, and if he ever did do so was rude and at no pains to conceal his contradictions. Also at a banquet given by the King of the Nabataeans, on some weighty golden crowns being presented to Caesar and Agrippina, and some light ones to Piso and the other guests, he was heard to remark that this feast was given to the son of a Eoman Prince not of a Parthian King. As he spoke he tossed away the crown and launched out into a long tirade against voluptuousness, which, though he submitted to it, galled Germanicus to the quick.

58. During these occurrences ambassadors ar-*Embassy of* rived from Artabanus, King of the Parthians.. He *Kot'* had sent them to remind Germanicus of their friendship and alliance, and to express his wish *Germani*to renew his engagements, offering out of deference to him to come to the banks of the Euphrates, and requesting in the meantime that Vonones should not be allowed an asylum in Syria, where his

agents could take advantage of their vicinity to foment dissensions among the Chieftains of the Tribes. In reply Germanicus spoke with full. appreciation of the alliance between Parthia and Eome, and of the King's visit and respect to himself personally with becoming diffidence. And he removed Vonones to Pompeiopolis, a seaport town of Cilicia. This was not more a concession to Artabanus than an affront to Piso, with whom Yonones had ingratiated himself by a number of attentions and presents with which he had won over Plancina. 59. In the consulship of Marcus Silanus and *Germani*Lucius Norbanus, Germanicus made an expedition *to Egypt into* Egypt to study its antiquities. The interests of J«X/j the province were however nominally his object, *TM?£"* and by throwing open the granaries he lowered *ifeappro* u ' t A A i the price ot corn, and assumed many popular *Tiberius.* habits, walking without guards, with sandals on his feet instead of shoes, and with a dress like that of the Greeks; thus imitating Publius Scipio, who, we have been told, constantly acted in the same manner in Sicily, even while the war with Carthage was still raging. Tiberius, mildly censuring his dress and deportment, bitterly inveighed against his having transgressed the ordinances of Augustus by entering Alexandria without permission of the Prince. For Augustus, among the other profundities of his system, had forbidden the Senators and Koman Knights of note to visit Egypt, sequestering it in order to take the means of starving Italy away from anyone who might seize this province with its keys both to sea and land, and defy a large army even with a small force.

60. But Germanicus, as yet ignorant that his *Egyptian* expedition excited disapproval, sailed up the Nile *Canopus,* Abookir. starting from Canopus. This town was founded *j* by the Spartans as a monument to their pilot, *Shanua.* Canopus, who was buried there when Menelaus, while returning to Greece, was driven far out of his course to the coast of Libya. From this place he paid a visit to the mouth of the river nearest to it. It is sacred to Hercules, and the natives declare that he was born among them and was the oldest of all of that name, which was adopted afterwards by others of like prowess. Carnac, Then he visited the vast relics of ancient Thebes, Abou? where were still visible inscriptions in Egyptian Gournda. characters upon massive obelisks attesting its former splendour. He ordered one of the oldest priests to expound this language of the past. And according to him 700,000 men capable of bearing arms had once dwelt there, and King Ehamses with this force had made himself master of Libya, Ethiopia, Media, Persia, Bactria, and Scythia, and had held sway over all the countries inhabited by the Syrians and Armenians and their neighbours the Cappadocians, which stretch from the Bithynian to the Lycian sea. There also were inscribed the taxes imposed on each nation, the treasure of gold and silver, the number of arms and horses, the offerings to the temples of ivory and spice, and the supplies of corn and all com modities which each nation was to contribute, on as grand a scale as the revenue raised at the present day by the strength of Parthia and the power of Rome.

61. Besides these Germanicus's attention was *statue of* attracted by other marvels, chief of which were ' the stone statue of Memnon, which emits a musical *pyj*note when the sunbeams fall on it; the pyramids, *reservoirs.* which seem like mountains reared amid shifting «nTc«««. and almost impassable sands by the rivalry and

Mareotis opulence of kings; the artificial lakes, reservoirs for

Mceris, the Nile's overflow; and in other places the river's

Birket narrowness and its vast depths which no soundandBirket ig fathomed. Thence he came to Elephantine and Syene, once the limits of the Eoman -

Empire, which now stretches to the Eed Sea.

62. During this summer, while Germanicus was *ihusus* passing from province to province, Drusus ac-*uwar* quired no small credit by tempting the Germans to *J* engage in civil war, and to strike a death-blow at *Catuaida dttacl's*

At the the already broken power of Maroboduus. There *Maroboy*thevi- among the Gotones a young chief called -

-Catualda, who had been once forcibly driven into exile by Maroboduus, and now when that king's fortunes were tottering, ventured on revenge.

With a strong force he marched into the territory

Bohemia, of the Marcomanni, and bribing the leading men

Prague? to join him, burst into the palace and the adjacent fort. In it were found all the pillage the Suevi had accumulated for long years, and some suttlers and traders, whom commercial advantages and afterwards lust of gain, finally forgetfulness of their fatherland, had lured from their own homes to become denizens of an enemy's soil.;

K 63. Maroboduus, abandoned on all sides, had *Marobo*nothing left but to throw himself on the pity of *applies to* Caesar. He crossed the Danube where it washes the province of Noricum and wrote to Tiberius *Kavenna,* not in the tone of a fugitive or a supplicant but *and Catu*in accordance with recollections of his former *expulsion* position. 'For, when he was a renowned king *coimtry*and had been invited by many nations to rule 2? over them, he had preferred the friendship of *J££* Eome.' Caesar's reply was that he should have a *transsecure* and honourable residence in Italy while *ydtht* he stayed there, and if anything else should be " more for his advantage he might go as freely *Vannius.* as he came. In a different tone Caesar declared to the senate 'that Philip was not so formidable to the Athenians, nor Pyrrhus and Antiochus so formidable to the Eomans as this man was.' The speech is still extant in which he magnified Maroboduus's importance, the ferocity of the nations under his sway, his alarming proximity to Italy if he were an enemy, and his own wisdom in compassing his overthrow. And certainly while Maroboduus lived at Eavenna his restoration always acted as a threat to the Suevi when they were insubordinate. But he never quitted Italy for eighteen years, and as he grew old lost much of his reputation from clinging inordinately to life. Catualda fared equally ill and sought the same asylum. He was soon afterwards driven out by the forces of the Hermunduri, headed by Vibilius and was taken under the protection of Eome and sent to Forum Julium, a colony of 'While Maroboduus.' Or it may mean, 'Maroboduus was kept at Ravenna.'

Narbonensian Gaul. The barbarian followers of both kings, for fear they might, if dispersed through the provinces, disturb their tranquillity, were established beyond the Danube between the

Morava? Marus and the Cusus, under the sovereignty of Vannius of the canton of the Quadi.

64. As soon as the news came of Artaxias *Honours to* being made king of Armenia by Germanicus, the *strife in* Senate passed a resolution that he and Drusus should enter the city with an ovation. Arches *Bhatm ports and* also were raised on each side of the temple of *Cotys.*

Mars Ultor, together with statues of the two

Cassars, and Tiberius was more pleased at having by policy secured peace than if by battle he had terminated a war. With these ideas he brought stratagem to bear also on Ehescuporis, King of Thrace. Ehcemetalces had been sole king of that nation, but at his death Augustus assigned half of it to Ehescuporis his brother, half to Cotys his son. In this partition the cultivated land and towns and the Greek frontier fell to Cotys, the waste and wild land with enemies on its border to

Ehescuporis. And the personal dispositions of the two kings were equally different. The former was amiable and agreeable, the latter grim and grasping, and unable to brook a divided sovereignty. At the outset, however, they maintained a hollow amity. But before long Ehescuporis began to encroach on the frontier and appropriate the share of Cotys, employing force where he met with resistance, but acting warily during

the life of Augustus, who, as he had planned the scheme to which each kingdom owed its origin, would, he feared, avenge any infraction of it.

But the moment he heard of the change of *Ehescu*sovereign he poured in gangs of brigands and *-treZker*demolished the forts as a provocation to war. c£ 65. Nothing harassed Tiberius so much as a *Tiberius summons* prospect of the derangement of order. He sent *Mm to* a Centurion expressly to forbid the two kings *cotys*and resorting to the decision of the sword. Upon which Cotys instantly dismissed the forces he had *Senates , ,, arbitra* raised. Ehescuporis with a show of fairness re-*tvm.*

quired a meeting where they could settle their differences by talking them over. They soon agreed when, where, and upon what terms it should be held, since from ductility on the one side, duplicity on the other, they were mutually yielding and compliant. Ehescuporis—to solemnise, as he insisted, the treaty—afterwards gave a banquet, and when the revel had been protracted far into the night and Cotys, what with the feasting and fumes of wine, was thrown off his guard,

loaded him with fetters. It was all in vain that when he comprehended the trick, he appealed to the inviolability of a king, the gods of the house of which they were both members, and the table at which he was his guest. And now being master of all Thrace, Ehescuporis wrote to Tiberius that a conspiracy had been hatched against himself, but that he had been beforehand with the conspirators.

And all the while, under the pretext of a war against the Basternas and Scythians he strengthened himself with fresh levies of infantry and cavalry. Tiberius calmly replied that if he had acted in good faith he might safely rely on his innocence; still neither he nor the Senate, without hearing the case, could decide on its rights

and wrongs. He must therefore surrender Cotys and shift from himself to him the odium of such a charge.

66. This letter Latinius Pandusa, pro-

praetor of *Murder of* Moesia, sent to Thrace along with a party of " soldiers to whom Cotys was to be surrendered. Ehescuporis, wavering between fear and rage, decided that it was better to be arraigned for the consummation than the commencement of a crime, and ordered Cotys to be executed, giving out that he had committed suicide. This, however, did not make Ca3sar lay aside his mask of conciliation now that he had assumed it, but on the death of Pandusa, whom Ehescuporis accused of personal hostility to him, he appointed to the government of Moesia Pomponius Flaccus, a veteran officer, whom he selected as an intimate friend of the King and therefore better qualified to entrap him.

67. Flaccus crossed over into Thrace, and by *shescu*lavish assurances prevailed on the King, though he *TM* j was distrustful and his heart misgave him for his «crimes, to present himself at the Eoman posts. *Some. T-t -.* T n i, p-i *Banished*

Here he was surrounded by a strong force under *to Aux*pretence of its being a guard of honour; and the ' tribunes and centurions by recommendations and *ff* persuasion, and by constraint the more undisguised *executed.* the farther they got away, conveyed him, aware *divided* at last that he was a prisoner, thence to Eome. *fTM* He was accused before the Senate by the wife of *talces and*

Cotys and sentenced to live in exile far from his *sons* kingdom. Thrace was divided between his son *Bufus' Ehoemetalces,* who, it was clearly proved, had *l* opposed his father's projects, and the children of 9i*Cotys.* And as they were not yet of age Tre bellienus Eufus was appointed trustee of the kingdom during their minority; on the precedent furnished by our ancestors who sent Marcus

Lepidus to iEgypt as guardian of Ptolemy's children. Ehescuporis was deported to Alexandria,

and there for attempting to escape, or falsely charged with doing so, was put to death.

68. About the same time Vonones, who as I *Vonones*

have related had been removed to Cilicia, bribed /nm" his jailers and attempted to escape to Armenia, 'Xl-v?

Derbend. thence to Albania, Heniochia, and the King of *Pyramtis.*

Scythia who was his kinsman. On pretext of *Remmius,* hunting he avoided the seaside district and made *supposed* for remote forest-passes, and after a time, thanks *zzds"",* jihan? to the swiftness of his horse, reached the Pyramus where the people of the neighbourhood had broken down the bridges on hearing of the King's flight, and where there was no ford. So that on the banks of the river he was seized by Vibius Fronto, a captain of cavalry, and soon afterwards Eemmius, an exempt, previously the King's keeper, pretending to be transported with passion, ran him through with his sword. This makes me more inclined to believe that he was an accomplice in his escape, and killed Vonones from fear of his betraying him. 69. Meanwhile Germanicus, on his return from Egypt, heard that all his arrangements, both in *q* the army and the towns, had been disregarded or , reversed. This made him put galling slights on *mints.* Piso, who assailed Cassar with equal virulence. *fageZl'* At last Piso resolved to leave Syria, but was soon detained by Germanicus falling ill. When he heard of his convalescence and that thanksgivings *pects Piso* were being offered for his escape, he sent lictors to *of sorcery,* disperse the victims when they were actually at *toning* the altars, the preparations for the sacrifice, and

Antaki. populace of Antioch amid their rejoicings.

Seiefke. Then he set off for Beleucia to await the issue of the disease, which had again attacked Germanicus. 'Ihe pangs of Germanicus's malady were made more acute by his conviction that he had been poisoned by Piso. Certainly there were found under the floor and walls disinterred relics of human bodies, incantations and spells, Germanicus's name engraved on sheets of lead, bones, half burned, and smeared with gore, and other sorceries by which it is supposed that a life is devoted to the infernal powers. At the same time Piso's emissaries were charged with prying into the unfavourable symptoms of the case.

70. This filled Germanicus, when he heard of *Piso* it, with as much indignation as alarm. 'If he *omttL*
was a prisoner in his own house, if he must breathe *p-*
out his life under his enemies' eyes, what would befall his unhappy wife and his tender babes when he was gone? Piso thought his drugs too slow.

He was in hot haste to gain sole command of the province and the army; but Germanicus was not yet so far gone, nor should the murderer reap the fruits of his crime.' He addressed a letter to Piso in which he renounced his friendship, and, most people say, ordered him to quit the province.

This Piso did without farther delay, but though he set sail, he regulated his speed so as to have the less distance to return in case the death of

Germanicus should have left Syria vacant.

71. For a short time Caesar was inclined to *Gemani*hope; but as his strength failed and his end drew *cue's* near he addressed his assembled friends to this *address to* effect. 'If I was dying a natural death I should have just cause for indignation, even against the gods, for snatching me away in the flower of my life by an untimely doom, from my parents, my little ones, and my country. But as it is the wickedness of Piso and Plancina by which I am cut off, I charge you to treasure up in your hearts these my last entreaties. Relate to my father and my brother the persecutions by which I have been tormented, the snares in which I have been entrapped, the wretchedness of my life, and the misery of the death which closed it. Those who in my lifetime were influenced by my prospects, by their relationship to me, nay, by their jealousy of me, will weep that one once so prosperous, who had survived so many wars, should fall by the arts of a woman. You will have an opportunity of complaining to the senate, of appealing to the laws. It is not the chief duty of a man's friends to follow him to the tomb with useless lamentations, but to remember his wishes, to execute his commands. Others who knew him not will mourn for Germanicus. Be it yours to avenge him! if it was myself and not my prosperity that you held dear. Show to the Eoman people her who is the granddaughter of the Immortal Augustus as well as my wife. Tell them the number of my six children. Their sympathy will be with the accusers; and if these wretches pretend that they only obeyed their orders, they will meet with no faith, certainly with no forgiveness.' Clasping the right hand of the dying man his friends swore that they would surrender their lives sooner than their revenge. 72. Then turning to his wife he entreated her

'by her affection for his memory, by the sons of *tobe* their love, to put away her proud spirit and stoop *f'* to the strokes of Fortune, and when she had .. *character.* returned to Eome, not provoke, by striving for the mastery, those who were stronger than herself.' This he spoke aloud, but he whispered something more, expressing, it was supposed, his mistrust of Tiberius. Not long afterwards he died, to the deep sorrow of the province and adjacent nations. Peoples and kings far away bewailed him, so potent had been his courtesy to allies and his humanity to foes. Commanding alike in his aspect and address he upheld the majesty and dignity of his exalted position without becoming obnoxious to others or overbearing himself.

73. There was no parade of effigies or any pro-*His* cession at his funeral, but praises and reminiscences *Umpired* of his great qualities in full measure. And there %*fathe* were some who compared his personal appearance *J* and age, and mode of death, and, as an additional *his being* circumstance, the vicinity of the country where it ' occurred, to the end of Alexander the Great.

For each was of a fine presence, each of splendid lineage, each was slightly over thirty years of age, each had perished by the treachery of a countryman in a foreign land. But Germanicus had been gentle to his friends, temperate in his pleasures, married only to one wife, the father only of legitimate children, Avithout being inferior to the other as a warrior though not so reckless, and though, after having shattered the strength of the Germans by a series of victories, he had been debarred from effecting their complete subjugation. For if he had possessed uncontrolled authority, if he had had the privilege and title of a king, he would have outstripped him in the race for military glory as easily as he had done in humanity, in self-command, and all other excellent qualities. His body before being burned lay stripped in the forum of Antioch, which was the place fixed for his burial. There was no decisive proof whether it showed any traces of poison or not. For everyone, as he was prejudiced by compassion for Germanicus, and preconceived mistrust or partiality for Piso, put different constructions on the symptoms.

74. The generals and other senators there pro-*Sentius* ceeded to deliberate about the appointment of a *Governor* governor of Syria. Others were not very urgent %, in their claims, but there was a long contest be-*Martina . to Borne.* tween Vibius Marsus and Cneius Sentius. At last Marsus yielded to Sentius as older and more strenuous in his suit. On being appointed, Sentius sent to Eome a poisoner, notorious in the province, named Martina, who was Plancina's bosom friend, at the requisition of Vitellius, Veranius, and the others who were framing a case for prosecution, as if the criminals were already arraigned. 75. As for Agrippina, though weak with weep-*Agrippina* ing and ill in health, she so chafed at aught that *J* might retard her revenge, that she embarked, j"? taking with her her children and the remains of *indecent -..,. , .. exultation.*
Germanicus, amid universal commiseration. 'For she was a woman, she was of the most exalted rank, and as a wife her brilliant lot had so recently always drawn upon her looks of homage and congratulation; and now she was bearing away in her bosom the ashes of the departed, knowing not whether she could avenge him, full of forebodings for herself, and cursed, even in the number of her children, through each of whom Fortune might stan Co. inflict a stroke.' Piso, meanwhile, while off Cos, was informed of Germanicus's death. In indecent exultation at the news, he offered sacrifice and visited the temples without putting any restraint on his own delight or that of the still more unblushing Plancina, who chose the occasion to throw off mourning for a sister and put on holiday dress.

76. Centurions kept flocking in with assurances *puo,sson* that the hearts of the soldiers yearned towards '*uTMto* Piso, and that he ought to re-enter a province of *TM?*
'*o r Home xn* which he had been arbitrarily deprived and which *stantiy,* was now without a head. This made him consider *enter on*
what he should do, and his son, Marcus Piso, ad- '
vised instant return to Eome. 'As yet his case was not at all desperate, and he need not be alarmed at impotent suspicions or idle rumours.
His quarrel with Germanicus might, perhaps, subject him to unpopularity but not to punishment,
and his enemies would have had ample compensation in his removal from the province; whereas,
if he went back to it the resistance of Sentius must entail civil war, and he could not depend on the support of the centurions and soldiers with whom the recollection of the Imperator himself, and their deep-rooted affection for the Caesars, would carry the day.'

77. Domitius Celer, an intimate friend, urged *D miliua* opposite considerations. 'He ought not to let the *Ceier Os*opportunity slip. Piso, not Sentius, was in com-*f* mand of Syria. In his hands had been placed the ' symbols of the Praetor's office and its authority, in his hands the army. If he were assailed by a foe, who would have a better right to oppose force to force than one who had been intrusted with vicegerent powers and special orders? He should also allow the scandal time to wear off. Even innocence could rarely bear up against the first burst of prejudice. Whereas, if he should keep his hold of the army and strengthen his position, many things might chance to turn out in his favour which no prudence could foresee. Are we to hasten to reach Eome along with the ashes of Germanicus, that Agrippina's lamentations and the hasty credulity of an insensate mob may destroy you without your being allowed one word in your defence? You have Augusta for your confederate, Caesar for your friend, but neither avowedly so, and none will lament Germanicus's death more ostentatiously than those who exult over it most.' 78. Without much difficulty Piso, with his *piso sends* natural imperiousness, was won over to their *sriad* view, and in a despatch to Tiberius he accused *? . troops,*

Germanicus ' of insubordination and arrogance, and *after* of getting him out of the way in order to facilitate *Manifesto* his ambitious plans. As for himself, in seeking to *Sermani*resume the command of the army, he was actuated ".
'*Itbertus.* by the same loyalty as when in command of it before.' Then at once he put Domitius on board a trireme with orders to keep clear of the coast and sail away from the island out to sea for Syria.

He enrolled in companies deserters as fast as they flocked in, armed suttlers, crossed to the mainland and seized a batch of recruits on their march to Syria, and wrote to the chief of Cilicia to send auxiliary contingents. And young Piso pushed on strenuously these preparations for war, though he had opposed engaging in it.

79. And thus it happened that they were coast-*His fleet* ing along Lycia and Pamphylia, when they were '*jzhp*met by the fleet with Agrippina on board, and *yTM-, '-* burning with hate, both at first cleared for action; ' '*Piso's* but as each was afraid of the other they got no *reply.* further than recriminations. And Marcus Vibius *fomrrTpt* warned Piso that he should answer for what he" had done at Eome. He ieeringly replied, he '""?
. *advertises* would appear as soon as ever the praetor appointed *Pt of* to investigate poisoning cases had given the

pri-*prepares* soner and the prosecutors notice of the trial. " Ladikiyeh. Meanwhile Domitius, landing at Laodicea, a town of Syria, made for the winter quarters of the sixth legion, which was supposed to be most available for lawless projects, but was forestalled by the general, Pacuvius. Sentius informed Piso of this by letter, and warned him not to tamper with the army or stir up a war in the province. Then he mustered all who were known to be loyal to the memory of Germanicus and opponents of his foes, and repeatedly impressing on them that an open attack was being made cn the majesty of the Imperator and on the commonwealth, led out a well-appointed force prepared for battle. 80. Piso, on his side, notwithstanding the mis-*puothrows* carriage of his first attempt, neglected no precau 'Jeeringly.' 'Evasively' according to Orelli. tions best adapted to his circumstances, but threw *imdreh.* himself into a strongly fortified fastness of Cilicia *futro,* Khelin-called Celendris. For by incorporating the Cilician contingents sent by the chiefs, with the deserters and the recruits he had recently seized, and with his own and Plancina's slaves, he had made them up to the number of a legion. And he gave out ' that he was Cassar's representative, that Caesar had set him over the province from which he was excluded, not by the army (at whose invitation, in fact, he was there), but by Sentius, who masked a personal grudge under lying imputations. They must form in battle array, and the soldiers would never fight when they saw Piso, whom they once called " Father," with rights that were incontestable, and might enough if he were obliged to assert them.' Then he made his companies deploy in front of the fortifications on a steep and precipitous hill, for the sea surrounded the other sides. He was confronted by veterans drawn up in ranks and reserves. One side had the most formidable men, the other the most formidable position, but neither heart nor hope, nor any except rustic weapons or clumsy makeshifts. When they came to blows the issue was doubtful only until the Eoman cohorts fought their way up to a. level with the foe. The Cilicians instantly took to flight and barricaded themselves within the fort. 81. While this was going on, Piso made an un- _ successful assault on the fleet which lav not far *?f 'attack on* off, and having by this time come back, he showed *the fleet.* !/ *h£S to* himself on the walls, and now by gestures of *seduce the* despair, now by appealing to individuals by name, *binaries* he attempted to stir up a mutiny by his promises, *from their* and had produced such an effect that one standard-*surrenders* bearer of the 6th legion went over to him. Then Sehtius ordered the clarions and bugles to strike *prepares to storm* up, materials to be fetched for an earthwork, *the fort.* scaling-ladders to be planted, a forlorn hope to be formed of volunteers under cover of a discharge of spears, stones, and fire-balls from the engines. At last Piso's stubbornness gave way, and he sued for permission to retain possession of the fort on surrendering his arms until application could be made to Caesar to decide who should be governor of Syria. His offer was not entertained, nor would they promise him aught but some ships and a safeconduct to Eome. 82. Meanwhile, at Eome, as "soon as it got *Wectsat* bruited about that Germanicus was ill, and as all *Germani*the reports, in proportion to the distance they travelled, came exaggerated for the worse, there was indignation and rage. Men even broke out *P f his re* into open murmurs. 'So this was why he had *covery.* been removed to those remote regions, why Piso had been appointed to the province; this was the result of Augusta's confidential colloquies with Plancina. Truly indeed had their fathers said of Drusus, " That it was odious in the eye of sovereigns for their sons to show popular instincts, and that they were cut off solely because they meditated giving back to the Eoman people freedom and comprehensive equality in the eye of the law."' These opinions of the populace were so intensified by news of Germanicus's death, that without waiting for the official proclamation, without waiting for the Senate's resolution, they voluntarily sus pended business, left the public places empty, and shut up their private houses. Silence or lamentation reigned throughout the city without any ostentatious parade, and though they could hot refrain from outward marks of mourning, their woe was more heartfelt. It happened that some traders who had left Syria before Germanicus's death brought some more cheering reports of his condition. They gained instant credit, instant publicity.

Everyone passed on the ill-authenticated intelligence to those he met, with joyous additions of his own, and they again to others. The whole city poured out and thronged to the entrance of the temples. Night made them more credulous,

and assertion became more confident in the dark.

Tiberius, however, gave no contradiction to the false report, till in course of time it died away.

83. This made the people more bitterly indig-*Honours* nant, as if Germanicus had been torn from them a second time. In proportion to their affection for him or their invention, they devised distinctions and carried them by decree—the introduction of his name into the words of the Salic chaunt; a chair of state among the priests of Augustus, and over it a crown of oak; the place of honour for a statue of him in ivory at the games of the circus; that his successors as flamen and augur should be chosen only out of the Julian family. In addition, arches at Eome, on the banks of the imadagh. Ehine and on Mount Amanus in Syria, with his exploits engraved on them, and his having died in the services of the state; a cenotaph at Antioch where he was burnt, a barrow at Epidaphna where he had died. No one easily could count the multitude of statues or the places where worship of them was established. On its being proposed to set up to him a golden shield of extraordinary size among the fathers of eloquence, Tiberius declared that he would dedicate one himself of the usual size and like the others, for rank lent eloquence no lustre, and it was high enough honour to be included among the old writers. The knights called their

seats in the theatre, which had hitherto been spoken of as belonging to the juniors, after Germanicus, and established a procession of squadrons behind his effigy on the fifteenth of July. There were many other things, some of which were abandoned at once or in process of time became obsolete. 84. But while their tears for Germanicus were *Smsm,s* yet flowing, his sister Livia, wife of Drusus, gave "*jly* birth to twin sons. This event so uncommon, and *fj'f* '*Disgust of* a matter of congratulation even in families of *the people.* humble means, made the prince so elated that he could not refrain from boasting before the senate that in the family of no Eoman of equal eminence had there been ever before two children at one birth. For it was his habit to claim everything— even if accidental—as reflecting credit on himself. But at such a time this excited fresh indignation among the people to whom the increase of Drusus's family seemed like an additional blow to the house of Germanicus. 85. The same year the senate passed stringent *Sumptuary* measures to check the licentiousness of women, *Tt'some.* and anyone whose grandfather or father or hus-J band had been a Eoman knight was forbidden to *s*

T . _ .... *ship of* gain her living by prostitution. For V istiha, who *his abolished.*

L was sprung from a praetorian family, had openly 4,000 *Jews* avowed her trade as a prostitute before the asdiles, *u Sar-* on the principle admitted among our ancestors " who considered women guilty of unchastity sufficiently punished by the mere avowal of their shame. Proceedings were also taken against Titidius Labeo, Vistilia's husband, for having neglected to put the law in force against his wife, though there was no doubt of her guilt. But on his pleading in excuse that the sixty days allowed for deliberation had not yet elapsed, it was deemed sufficient to pass sentence on Vistilia, and she was

Scrpho. sent out of sight to the island of Seriphos. The Egyptian rites and the expulsion of the Jews also came under consideration, and the senate passed a resolution for carrying to the island of Sardinia four thousand of the class of freedmen fit for service who were tainted with that fanaticism in order to quell brigandage in the island, as even if they perished from the pestilential climate it would be no great loss: the rest were to evacuate Italy if by a stated day they had not abandoned their unholy ceremonies.

86. Then Cassar gave notice that a virgin must *Poiiw's* be elected in the room of Occia, who for fifty-seven $1 years had been in charge of the vestal worship, and he expressed his gratitude to Fonteius Agrippa *place of* and Domitius Pollio for patriotic emulation in tendering their daughters. Pollio's daughter was preferred solely because her mother had never been parted from her husband, for Agrippa had slurred the family credit by divorcing his wife. But though she was rejected, Cassar, as a consolation, 8,333 e 1 presented her with a dowry of a million sesterces.

87, As the populace complained of the cruel *TOmm's* price of provisions, Tiberius fixed the price which *jjjZ.'* the purchaser was to pay for corn, engaging to pay out of his own purse two additional sesterces j per bushel to the sellers. He would not, however, *at being* any the more accept the title of father of his *dominus.'* country now offered him, not for the first time, and sharply rebuked persons who had spoken of his 'godlike functions' and of himself as ' Master.' So that choice of words became circumscribed and hazardous under a prince who dreaded freedom and detested sycophancy. 88. I find in the writings of contemporary *Mgan*historians and senators that a letter was read in *fferlTo* the senate from Adgandestrius, chief of the Chatti, XtTM// in which he undertook to assassinate Arminius if Jf *noble* he was supplied with poison to do the deed, and *answer.* that it was replied that it was not by treachery Or *character* in the dark, but in the face of day and in arms, *inius.* that the people of Borne took vengeance upon their foes. A noble answer, by which Tiberius c. Fabri-raised himself to the level of those commanders of old who had repulsed and disclosed to Pyrrhus the plot to poison him. As for Arminius, on the departure of the Eomans and the expulsion of Maroboduus, he aspired to the throne and became the foe of his countrymen's freedom, and when, they made war on him maintained a chequered contest with them, till he perished by the treachery of his kinsmen. Beyond all question he was the emancipator of Germany and one who defied Bome, not in her infancy as other kings and commanders did, but in the full splendour of her empire, and though not invariably successful in battle, invincible in a war. He completed the thirty-seventh year of his age and the twelfth of his supremacy, and still lives in the songs of the barbarians, unnoticed in the histories of Greek writers who appreciate only their own exploits, and among us Eomans inadequately famous, indifferent as we are to the present amid our eulogies of the past. 39 Paternoster Row, E.C.

London: *November* 1872.

GENERAL LIST OF' WORKS PUBLISHED BY

Messrs. IM&MAIS, GKREM, READER, and DYER.

Arts, Manotactubes, &c 13
Astronomy, Meteorology, Popular Geogbaphy, &e 8
BLOGBaPHICAL WOBKS 4
Chemistry, Medicine, Subgery, and the Allied Sciences 11
Criticism, Philosophy, Polity, &c.... 5
Fine Abts and Illustrated Editions 12
Histoby, Politics, and Historical Memoirs 1
Index 21—24
Knowledge for the Young 20
Miscellaneous Works and Popular Metaphysics 6
Natural History & Popular Science 9
Periodical Publications 20
Poetry and The Drama 18
Religious and Moral Works 14
Rural Sports, &c 19
Travels, Voyages, &c 16
Works of Fiction 17
Works of Utility and General Information IS *History, Politics, Historical Memoirs, fyc.*

Estimates of the English Kings from William the Conqueror to George III. By J. Langton Sanford, Author of 'Studies anil Illustrations of the Great Rebellion' &c. Crown 8vo. price 12s. Gd.

The History of England from the Fall of Wolsey to the Defeat of the Spanish Armada. By James Anthony Froude, M. A.

Cabinet Edition, 12 vols. cr. 8vo. £3 12s.

Library Edition, 12 vols. 8vo. £8 18s.

The English in Ireland in the Eighteenth Century. By James Anthony Froude, M.A. late Fellow of Exeter College, Oxford. In Two Volumes. Vol. I, 8vo. price 16s.

The History of England from the Accession of James II. By Lord Macaulay:—

Student's Edition, 2 vols, crown 8vo. 12s.

People's Edition, 4 vols, crown 8vo. 16s.

Cabinet Edition, 8 vols, post 8vo. 48s.

Library Edition, 5 vols. 8vo. £4.

Lord Macaulay's Works. Complete and uniform Library Edition. Edited by his Sister, Lady Trevelyan. 8 vols. 8vo. with Portrait, price £5. 5s. cloth, or £8. 8s. bound in tree-calf by Riviere.

Memoirs of Baron Stockmar. By his Son, Baron E. von Stockmar. Translated from the German by G. A. M. Edited by Max Muller, M.A. 2 vols, crown 8vo. price 21s.

Varieties of Vice-Regal Life. By Major-General Sir William Denison, K.C.B. late Governor-General of the Australian Colonies, and Governor of Madras. With Two Maps. 2 vols. 8vo. 28s.

On Parliamentary Government in England: its Origin, Development, and Practical Operation. By Alpheus Todd, Librarian of the Legislative Assembly of Canada. 2 vols. 8vo. price £1. 17s.

The Constitutional History of England since the Accession of George III. 1760—1860. By Sir Thomas Erskine May, K.C.B. Cabinet Edition (the Third), thoroughly revised. 3 vols, crown 8vo. price 18s.

A Historical Account of the Neutrality of Great Britain during the American Civil War. By Mountagce Bernard, M. A. Royal 8vo. price 16s.

The History of England, from the Earliest Times to the Year 1865. By C. D. Yonge, Regius Professor of Modern History in Queen's College, Belfast. New Edition. Crown 8vo. 7s. Gd. 2 NEW WORKS PUBLIShed Ry LONGMANS And CO.

Lectures on the History of England, from the Earliest Times to the Death of King Edward II. By William LongMan. With Maps and Illustrations. 6vo. 15j.

The History of the Life andTimes of Edward the Third. By William Longman. With 9 Maps, 8 Plates, and 16 Woodcuts. 2 vols. 8vo. 28s.

History of Civilization in England and France, Spain and Scotland. By Henry Thomas Buckle. New Edition of the entire work, with a complete Index. 8 vols, crown 8vo. 24s.

Realities of Irish Life. By W. Steuart Trench, Land Agent in Ireland to the Marquess of Lansdowne, the Marquess of Bath, and Lord Digby. Fifth Edition. Crown 8vo. 6s.

The Student's Manual of the History of Ireland. By M. F. Cusack, Authoress of 'The Illustrated History of Ireland.' Crown 8vo. price 6s.

A Student's Manual of the History of India, from the Earliest Period to the Present. By Colonel Meadows TayLor, M.R.A.S. M.K.I.A. Crown 8vo. with Maps, 7s. 6d.

The History of India, from the Earliest Period to the close of Lord Dalhousie's Administration. By John Clark Marshman. 3 vols, crown 8vo. 22s. Gd.

Indian Polity; a View of the System of Administration in India. By Lieut-Col. George Chesney. Second Edition, revised, with Map. 8vo. 21s.

A Colonist on the Colonial Question. By Jehu Mathews, of Toronto, Canada. Post 8vo. price 6s.

An Historical View of Literature and Art in Great Britain from the Accession of the House of Hanover to the Beign of QueenVictoria. By J. Murray Graham, M.A. 8vo. price 14s.

Waterloo Lectures: a Study of the Campaign of 1815. By Colonel Charles C. Chesney, K.E. late Professor of Military Art and History in the Staff College. Second Edition. 8vo. with Map, 10s. 6t

Memoir and Correspondence relating to Political Occurrences in June and July 1834. By Edward John Littleton, First Lord Hatherton. Edited, from the Original Manuscript, by Henry Reeve, C.B. D.C.L. 8vo. price 7s. 64

Chapters from French History; St. Louis, Joan of Arc, Henri IV. with Sketches of the Intermediate Periods. By J. H. Gurney, M.A. New Edition. Fcp. 8vo. 6s. Gd.

History of the Reformation in Europe in the Time of Calvin. By J. H. Merle D'aurigne,, D.D. Vols. L and II. 8vo. 28s. Vol. III. 12s. Vol. IV. price 16s. and Vol. V. price 16s.

Royal and Republican Prance. A Series of Essays reprinted from the 'Edinburgh,,' Quarterly,' and 'British and Foreign, Reviews. By Henry Reeve, O.B. D.C.L. 2 vols. 8vo. price 21s.

The Imperial and Colonial Constitutions of the Britannic Empire, including Indian Institutions. By Sir Edward Creasy, M.A. &c. With Six Maps. 8vo. price 15s.

Home Politics: being a Consideration of the Causes of the Growth of Trade in relation to Labour, Pauperism, and Emigration. By Daniel Grant. 8vo. 7s.

The Oxford Reformers—John Colet, Erasmus, and Thomas More; being a History of their Fellow-Work. By Frederic Seerohm. Second Edition. 8vo. 14s.

The History of Greece. ByC. THiRLwall, D.D. Lord Bishop of St. David's. 8 vols. fcp. 28s.

The Tale of the Great Persian War, from the Histories of Herodotus. By George W. Cox, M.A. late Scholar of Trin. Coll. Oxon. Fcp. 3s. Gd.

The Sixth Oriental Monarchy; or, the History, Geography, and Antiquities of Parthia. Collected and Blustrated from Ancient and Modern sources. By George Rawxinson, M.A. Camden Professor of Ancient History in the University of Oxford, and Canon of Canterbury. 8vo. with Maps and Illustrations. *'Nearly ready.*

Greek History from Themistocles to Alexander, in a Series of Lives from Plutarch. Revised and arranged by A. H. Clough. Fcp. with 44 Woodcuts, 6s.

Critical History of the Language and Literature of Ancient Greece. By William Mure, of Caldwell. 5 vols. 8vo. £3 9s.

History of the Literature of Ancient Greece. By Professor K.o. moller. Translated by Lewis and Donaldson. 3 vols. 8vo. 21.

The History of Borne. By Wilhelm Iitne. English Edition, translated and revised by the Author. Vols. I. and II. 8vo. 30s.

History of the City of Borne from its Foundation to the Sixteenth Century of the Christian Era. By Thomas H. Dyer, LL.D. 8vo. with 2 Maps, 15s.

History of the Bomans under , the Empire. By Very Rev. Charles Merivale.d.c.l. Dean of Ely. 8 vols, post 8vo. price 48s.

The Fall of the Boman Be publie; a Short History of the Last Century of the Commonwealth. By the same Author. 12mo. 7s. Gd.

Encyclopaedia of Chronology, Historical and Biographical: comprising the Dates of all the Great Events of History, including Treaties, Alliances, Wars, Battles, &c.; Incidents in the Lives of Eminent Men, Scientific and Geographical Discoveries, Mechanical Inventions, and Social, Domestic, and Economical Improvements. By B. B. Woodward, B.A. and W. L. R. Cates. 8vo. price 42s.

History of European Morals from Augustus to Charlemagne. By W. E. H. Lecky, M.A. 2 vols. 8vo. price 28s.

History of the Rise arid Influence of the Spirit of Rationalism in Europe. By the same Author. Cabinet Edition (the Fourth). 2 vols, crown 8vo. price lCs.

God in History; or, the Progress of Man's Faith in the Moral Order of the World. By the late Baron Bunsen. Translated from the German by Susanna WinkWorth; with a Preface by Dean Stanley. 3 vols. 8vo. 42s.

Socrates and the Socratic Schools. Translated from the German of Dr. E. ZelLer, with the Author's approval, by the Rev. Oswald J. Reichel, B.C.L. and M.A. Crown 8vo. 8s. Gd.

The Stoics, Epicureans, and Sceptics. Translated from the German of Dr. E. Zeller, with the Author's approval, by Oswald J. Reichel, B.C.L. and M.A. Crown 8vo. 14s. The English Beformation. By F. C. Massingberd, M. A. Chancellor of Lincoln. 4th Edition, revised. Fcp. 7s. Gd.

Three Centuries of Modern History. By Charles Duke Yonge, Regius Professor of Modern History and English Literature in Queen's College, Belfast. Crown 8vo. 7s. Gd.

Saint-Simon and Saint-Simonism; a Chapter in the History of Socialism in France. By Arthur J. Booth, M.A. Crown 8vo. price 7s. Gd.

The History of Philosophy, from Thales to Comte. By George Henry Lewes. Fourth Edition, corrected, and partly rewritten. 2 vols. 8vo. 32s.

The Mythology of the Aryan Nations. By George W. Cox, M.A. late Scholar of Trinity College, Oxford. 2 vols. 8vo. price 28s.

Maunder's Historical Treasury; comprising a General Introductory Outline of Universal History, and a Series of Separate Histories. Fcp. 8vo. price 6s.

Critical and Historical Essays contributed to the *Edinburgh Review* by the Right Hon. Lord Macaulay:—

Student's Edition, crown 8vo. 6s.

People's Edition, 2 vols, crown 8vo. 8s.

Cabinet Edition, 4 vols. 24».

Library Edition, 3 vols. 8vo. 36s.

History of the Early Church, from the First Preaching of the Gospel to the Council of Nicasa, A.d. 325. By the Author of 'Amy Herbert.' New Edition. Fcp. 4s. 64

Sketch of the History of the Church of England to the Revolution of 1688. By the Right Rev. T. V. Short, D.D. Lord Bishop of St. Asaph. Eighth Edition. Crown 8vo. 7s. Gd.

History of the Christian Church, from the Ascension of Christ to the Conversion of Constantine. By E. Burton, D. D. late Regius Prof, of Divinity in the University of Oxford. Fcp. 3s. Gd.

History of the Christian Church, from the Death of St. John to the Middle of the Second Century; comprising a full Account of the Primitive Organisation of Church Government, and the Growth of Episcopacy. By T. W. Mossman, B. A. Rector of East and Vicar of West Torrington, Lincolnshire. 8vo. *In the press.*

Iiifeof Alexander von Humboldt. Compiled, in Commemoration of the Centenary of his Birth, by Julius LowenUkrg, Rorert Ave-lallemant, and Alfred Uove. Edited by Professor Karl Bruhns, Director of the Observatory at Leipzig. Translated from the German by Jane and Caroline Lassell. 2 vols. 8Vo. with Three Portraits. *Nearly ready.*

Autobiography of John Milton; or, Milton's Life in his own Words. By the Rev. James J. G. Graham, M.A. Crown 8vo. with Vignette-Portrait, price 5s.

Ba collections of Past Life. By Sir Henry Holland, Bart. M.D. F.R. S., &c. Physician-in-Ordinary to the Queen. Second Edition. Post 8vp. 10s. 5d.

Biographical and Critical Essays. By A. Hayward, Esq., Q.C. A New Series. 2 vols. 8vo. *In the press.*

The Life of Isambard Kingdom Brunei, Civil Engineer. By Isamrard Brunel, B.C.L. of Lincoln's Inn, Chancellor of the Diocese of Ely. With Portrait, Plates, and Woodcuts. 8vo. 21s.

Lord George Bentinck; a Political Biography. By the Right Hon. B. DisRaeli, M.P. Eighth Edition, revised, with a new Preface. Crown 8vo. *Gs.*

The Life and Letters of the Rev. Sydney Smith. Edited by his Daughter, Lady Holland, and Mrs. Austin. New Edition, complete in One Volume. Crown 8vo. price 6s.

Memoir of George Edward Lynch Cotton, D.D. Bishop of Calcutta, and Metropolitan. With Selections from his Journals and Correspondence. Edited by Mrs. Ctton. New Edition. Crown 8vo. *Just ready.*

The Life and Travels of George Whitelield, M.A. By James Patersi N Gledstone. 8vo. price *Us.*

The Life and Times of Sixtus the Fifth. By Baron Hurner. Translated from the Original French, with the

Author,s sanction, by Hurert E. H. Jerningham. 2 vols. 8vo. 24s.

Essays in Ecclesiastical Biography. By the Right Hon. Sir J. Stephen, LL.D. Cabinet Edition. Crown 8vo. 7s. *Gd.*

Father Mathew; a Biography. By John Francis Maguire, M.P. Popular Edition, with Portrait. Crown 8vo. 3s. *Gd.*

The Life and Letters of Faraday. By Dr. Bence Jones, Secretary of the Royal Institution. Second Edition, with Portrait and Woodcuts. 2 vols. 8vo. 28s.

Faraday as a Discoverer. By John Tyndall, LL.D. F.R.S. New and Cheaper Edition, with Two Portraits. Fcp. 8vo price 3s. *Gd.*

The Royal Institution: its Founder and its First Professors. By Dr. Bence Jones, Honorary Secretary. Post 8vo. price 12s. 6rf.

Leaders of Public Opinion in Ireland; Swift, Flood, Grattan, O,Connell. By W. E. H. Lecky, M.A. New Edition, revised and enlarged. Crown 8vo. 7s. *Gd.*

A Group of Englishmen (1795 to 1815); Records of the Younger Wedgwoods and their Friends, embracing the History of the Discovery of Photography. By Eliza Meteyard. 8vo. Igs.

Life of the Duke of Wellington. By the Rev. G. R. Gleig, M.A. Popular Edition, carefully revised; with copious Additions. Crown 8vo. with Portrait, 5s.

Dictionary of General Biography; containing Concise Memoirs and Notices of the most Eminent Persons of all Countries, from the Earliest Ages to the Present Time. Edited by William L. R. Cates. 8vo. price 21s.

Letters and Life of Francis Bacon, including all his Occasional Works. Collected and edited, with a Commentary, by J. Spedding. Vols. I. to VI. 8vo. price £3.12s. To be completed in One more Volume.

Felix Mendelssohn's Letters from *Italy and Switzerland,* and *Letters* from 1833 to 1847, translated by Lady Wallace. With Portrait. 2 vols, crown 8vo. 5s. each.

Musical Criticism and Biography. Selected from the Published and Unpublished Writings of Thomas Damast Eaton, late President of the Norwich Choral Society. Edited by his Sons. Crown 8vo.

Lives of the Queens of England. By Agnes Strickland. Library Edition, newly revised; with Portraits of every Queen, Autographs, and Vignettes. 8 vols, post 8vo. 7s. *Gd.* each.

On Representative Government. By John Stuart Mill. Third Edition. 8vo. 9s. crown 8vo. 2s.

On Liberty. By the same Author. Fourth Edition. Post 8vo. 7s. *Gd.* Crown 8vo. 1s. *id.*

Principles of Political Economy. By the same. Seventh Edition. 2 vols. 8vo. 30s. or in 1 vol. crown 8vo. 5s.

Utilitarianism. By the same. 4th Edit. 8vo. 6s.

Dissertations and Discussions. By the same Author. Second Edition. 3 vols. 8vo. price 36s.

Examination of Sir W. Hamilton's Philosophy, and of the principal Philosophical Questions discussed in his Writings. By the same. Third Edition. 8vo. 16s.

The Subjection of Women. By John Stuart Mill. New Edition. Post 8vo. 5s.

Analysis of the Phenomena of the Human Mind. By James Mill. A New Edition, with Notes, Illustrative and Critical, *by* Alexander Bain, Andrew Find Later, and George Grote. Edited, with additional Notes, by John Stuart Mill. 2 vols. 8vo. price 28s.

Principles of Political Philosophy; being the Second Edition, revised and extended, of ' The Elements of Political Economy., By H. D. Macleod, M.A., Barrister-at-Law. In Two Volumes. Vol. I. 8vo. price 15s.

A Dictionary of Political Economy; Biographical, Bibliographical, Historical, and Practical. By the same Author. Vol. I. royal 8vo. 30s.

A Systematic View of the Science of Jurisprudence. By Sheldon Amos, M.A. Professor of Jurisprudence, University College, London. 8vo. price 18s.

The Institutes of Justinian; with English Introduction, Translation, and Notes. By T. C. Sandars, M.A. Barristerat-Law. New Edition. 8vo. 15s.

Lord Bacon's Works, collected and edited by R. L. Ellis, M.A. J. SpedDing, M.A. and D. D. Heath. New and Cheaper Edition. 7 vols. 8vo. price £3. 13s. *Gd.*

A System of Logic, Ratiocinative and Inductive. By John Stuart Mill. Eighth Edition. 2 vols. 8vo. 25s.

The Ethics of Aristotle; with Essays and Notes. By Sir A. Grant, Bart. M.A. LL.D. Third Edition, revised and partly re-written. _*In the press.*

The Micomachean Ethics of Aristotle. Newly translated into English. By K. Williams, BA. Fellow and late Lecturer Merton College, Oxford. 8vo. 12s.

Bacon's Essays, with Annotations. By R. Whately, D.D. late Archbishop of Dublin. Sixth Edition. 8vo. 10s. *Gd.*

Elements of Logic. By R. Whately, D.D. late Archbishop of Dublin. New Edition. 8vo. 10s. *Gd.* crown 8vo. 4s. *Gd.*

Elements of Rhetoric. By the same Author. New Edition. 8vo. 10s. 6d. Crown 8vo. 4s. *Gd.*

English Synonymes. ByE. Jane Whately. Edited by Archbishop Whately. 5th Edition. Fcp. 3s.

An Outline of the Necessary Laws of Thought: a Treatise on Pure and Applied Logic. By the Most Rev. W. Thomson, D.D. Archbishop of York. Ninth Thousand. Crown 8vo. 5s. *Gd.*

Causality; or, the Philosophy of Law Investigated. By George Jamieson, B.D. of Old Maeliar. Second Edition, greatly enlarged, tvo. price 12s.

Speeches of the Right Hon. Lord Macaulay, corrected by Himself. People,s Edition, crown 8vo. 3s. *Gd.*

Lord Macaulay's Speeches on Parliamentary Reform in 1831 and 1832. 16mo. price One Shilling.

A Dictionary of the English Language. Iiy R. G. Latham, M.A. M.D. F.R.S. Founded on the Dictionary of Dr. S. Johnson, as edited by the Rev. H. J. Todd, with numerous Emendations and Additions. 4 vols. 4to. price £7.

Thesaurus of English Words and Phrases, classified and arranged so as to facilitate the expression of Ideas, and assist in Literary Composition. By P. M. Roget, M.D. New Edition. Crown 8vo. 10s. Gd.

Three Centuries of English Literature. By Charles Dcke Yonge, Regius Professor of Modern History and English Literature in Queen,s College, Belfast. Crown 8vo. 7s. Gd.

Lectures on the Science of Language. By F. Max Muller, M.A. &c. Foreign Member of the French Institute. Sixth Edition. 2 vols, crown 8vo. price 16.

Chapters on Language. By F. W. Farrar, M.A. F.R.S. Head Master of Marlborough College. Crown 8vo. 8s. Gd.

Southey'S Doctor, complete in One Volume, edited by the Rev. J. W. Warter, B.D. Square crown 8vo. 12s. Gd.

Manual of English Literature, Historical and Critical with a Chapter on English Metres. By Thomas Arnold, M.A. Second Edition. Crown 8vo. 7s. Gd.

A Latin-English Dictionary. By John T. Wnite, D.D. Oxon. and J. E. Riddle, M.A. Oxon. Third Edition, revised. 2 vols. 4to. pp. 2,128, price 42s.

White's College Latin-English Dictionary (Intermediate Size), abridged from the Parent Work for the use of University Students. Medium 8vo. pp. 1,048, price 18s.

White's Junior Student's Complete Latin-English and English-Latin Dictionary.
Revised Edition. Square 12mo. pp. 1,058,
price 12s.
Senaratelv /english-lath?, 5s. Gd. Latin-english, 7s. Gd.

An English-Greek Lexicon, containing all the Greek Words used by Writers of good authority. By C. D. Y#nge, B. A. New Edition. 4to. 21s.

Mr. Yonge's New Lexicon, English and Greek, abridged from his larger work (as above). Square 12mo. 8s. Gd.

A Greek-English Lexicon. Compiled by II. G. Liddell, D.D. Dean of Christ Church, and R. Scott, D.D. Dean of Rochester. Sixth Edition. Crown 4to. price 36s.

A Lexicon, Greek and English, abridged for Schools from Liddell and Scott's *Greei-English Lexicon.* Fourteenth Edition. Square 12mo. 7s. Gd.

The Mastery of Languages; or, the Art of Speaking Foreign Tongues Idiomatically. By Thomas Prendergast, late of the Civil Service at Madras. Second Edition. 8vo. 6s.

A Practical Dictionary of the French and English Languages. By Professor Leon Contanseau, many years French Examiner for Military and Civil Appointments, &c. New Edition, carefully revised. Post 8vo. 10s. Gd.

Contanseau's Pocket Dictionary, French and English, abridged from the Practical Dictionary, by the Author. New Edition. 18mo. price 3s. Gd.

A Sanskrit-English Dictionary. The Sanskrit words printed both in the original Devanagari and in Roman letters; with References to the Best Editions of Sanskrit Authors, and with Etymologies and comparisons of Cognate Words chiefly in Greek, Latin, Gothic, and Anglo-Saxon. Compiled by T. Benfey. 8vo. 52s. Gd.

New Practical Dictionary of the German Language; German-English, and English-German. By the Rev. W. L. Blackley, M.A. and Dr. Carl Martin Friedlander. Post 8vo. 7s. Gd.

Historical and Critical Commentary on the Old Testament; with a New Translation. By M. M. KaLisch, Ph.D Vol. I. *Genesis,* 8vo. 18s. or adapted for the General Reader, 12s. Vol. II. *Exodus,* 15s or adapted for the General Reader, 12s. Vol III. *Leviticus,* Part I. 15s. or adapted for the General Reader, 8s. Vol. IV. *Leviticus,* Part II. 15s. or adapted for the General Reader, 8s.

A Hebrew Grammar, with Exercises. By the same. Part I. *Outlines with Exercises,* 8vo. 12s. Gd. Key, 5s. Part II. *Exceptional Forms and Constructions,* 12s. Gd. *Miscellaneous Works* and *Popular Metaphysics.*

An Introduction to Mental Philosophy, on the Inductive Method. By J. D. Morell, M.A. LL.D. 8vo. 12s.

Elements of Psychology, containing the Analysis of the Intellectual Powers. By J. D. Morell, LL.D. Post 8vo. 7s. Gd.

Recreations of a Country Parson. By A. K. H. B. Two Series, *3s. Gd.* each.

Seaside Musings on Sundays and Weekdays. By A. K. H. B. Crown 8vo. price 3s. Gd.

Present-Day Thoughts. By A. K. H. B. "Crown 8vo. 3s. *Gd.*

Changed Aspects of Unchanged Truths; Memorials of St. Andrews Sundays. By A. K. H. B. Crown 8vo. 3s. Gd.

Counsel and Comfort from a City Pulpit. By A. K. H. B Crown 8vo. 3s. Gd.

Lessons of Middle Age, with some Account of various Cities and Men. By A. K. H. B. Crown 8vo. 3«. Gd.

Leisure Hours in Town; Essays Consolatory, jEsthetical, Moral, Social, and Domestic. By A. K. H. B. Crown 8vo. 3s. Gd.

Sunday Afternoons at the Parish Church of a Scottish University City. By A. K. H. B. Crown 8vo. 3s. Gd.

The Commonplace Philosopher in Town and Country. By A. K. H. B. 3s. Gd.

The Autumn Holidays of a Country Parson. By A. K. H. B. Crown 8vo. 3s. Gd.

Critical Essays of a Country Parson. By A, K. H. B. Crown 8vo. 3s. Gd.

The Graver Thoughts of a Country Parson. By A. K. H. B. Two Series, 3s. Gd. each.

Miscellaneous and Posthumous Works of the late Henry Thomas Buckle. Edited, with a Biographical Notice by Helen Taylor. 3 vols. 8vo. price *11.12s. Gd.*

Short Studies on Great Subjects. By James Anthony Froude, M.A. late Fellow of Exeter College, Oxford. 2 vols, crown 8vo. price 12s.

Miscellaneous Writings of John Conington, M.A. late Corpus Professor of Latin in the University of Oxford. Edited by J. A. Symonds, M.A. With a Memoir by H. J. S. Smith, M.A. LL.D. F.ILS. 2 vols. 8vo. price 28s.

The Rev. Sydney Smith's Miscellaneous Works. 1 vol. crown 8vo. 6s.

The Wit and "Wisdom of the Eev. : Sydney Smith; a Selection of the most memorable Passages in his Writings and Conversation. Crown 8vo. 3s. Gd.

The Eclipse of Faith; or, a Visit to a ReHgious Sceptic. By Heney-Rogers. Twelfth Edition. Fcp. 8vo. 5s.

Defence of the Eclipse of Faith, by its Author. Third Edition. Fcp. 8vo. 3s. Gd.

Lord Macaulay's Miscellaneous Writings:— Library Edition, 2 vols. 8vo. Portrait, 21s. People's Edition, 1 vol. crown 8vo. 4s. Gd.

Lord Macaulay's Miscellaneous Writings and Speeches. Student's Edition, in One Volume, crown 8vo. price Gi.

Families of Speech, Four Lectures delivered at the Royal Institution of Great Britain. By the Rev. F. W. Farrar, M.A. F.R.S. Post 8vo. with 2 Maps, 5s. Gd.

Chips from a German Workshop; being Essays on the Science of Religion, and on Mythology, Traditions, and Customs. By F. Max Msller, M.A. &c. Foreign Member of the French Institute. 3 vols. 8to. £2.

A Budget of Paradoxes. By Augustus De Morgan, F.R.A.S. and C.P.S. of Trinity College, Cambridge. Reprinted, with the Author's Additions, from the *Athevceum*. 8vo. price 15s.

The Secret of Hegel: being the Hegelian System in Origin, Principle, Form, and Matter. By James Hutchison StirLing. 2 vols. 8vo. 28s.

Sir WiUiam Hamilton; being the Philosophy of Perception: an Analysis. By James Hutchison Stirling. 8vo. 5s.

As Regards Protoplasm. By J. H. Stirling, LL.D. Second Edition, with Additions, in reference to Mr. Huxley's Second Issue and a new Preface in reply to Mr. Huxley in 'Yeast.' 8vo. price 2s.

TTeberweg's System of Logic, and History of Logical Doctrines. Translated, with Notes and Appendices, by T. M. Lindsay, M.A. F.R.S.E. 8vo. price 16s.

The Philosophy of Necessity; or, Natural Law as applicable to Mental, Moral, and Social Science. By Charles Bray. Second Edition. 8vo. 9s.

A Manual of Anthropology, or Science of Man, based on Modern Research. By the same Author. Crown 8vo. 6s.

On Force, its Mental and Moral Correlates. By the same Author. 8vo. 5s.

The Discovery of a *New* World of Being. By George Thomson. Post 8vo. 6s.

Time and Space; a Metaphysical Essay. By Shadworth H. Hodgson. 8vo. price 16s.

The Theory of Practice; an Ethical Inquiry. By Shadworth H. Hodgson 2 vols. 8vo. price 24s.

Outlines of Astronomy. By Sir J. F. W. Hersciiel, Bart. M.A. Eleventh Edition, with 9 Plates and numerous Diagrams. Square crown 8vo. 12s.

Essays on Astronomy. A Series of Papers on Planets and Meteors, the Sun and sun surrounding Space, Stars and Star Cloudlets; and a Dissertation tin the approaching Transit of Venus: preceded by a Sketch of the Life and Work of Sir" J. Herschel. By R. A. Proctor, B.A. With 10 Plates and 24 Woodcuts. 8vo. price 12s.

Schellen's Spectrum Analysis, in its Application to Terrestrial Substances and the Physical Constitution of the Heavenly Bodies. Translated by Jane and C. Lassell; edited, with Notes, by W. Huggins, LL.D. F.R.S. With 13 Plates (6 coloured) and 223 Woodcuts. 8o. 28s.

The Sun; Ruler, Light, Fire, and Life of the Planetary System. By Richard A. Proctor, B.A. F.R.A.S. Second Edition; with 10 Plates (7 coloured) and 107 Woodcuts. Crown 8vo. price 14s.

Saturn and its System. By the same Author. 8vo. with 14 Plates, 14s.

Magnetism and Deviation of the Compass. For the use of Students in Navigation and Science Schools. By John Meruifield, LL.D. F.R.A.S. With Diagrams. 18mo. price 1s. Gd.

Navigation and Nautical Astronomy (Practical, Theoretical, Scientific) for the use of Students and Practical Men. By J. Merrifield, F.R.A.S. and H. Evers. 8vo. 14s.

Air and Bain; the Beginnings of a Chemical Climatology. By Rorert Angus Smith, Ph.D. F.R.S. F.C.S. Government Inspector of Alkali Works, with 8 Illustrations. 8vo. price 24s.

The Star Depths; or, other Suns than Ours; a Treatise on Stars, Star-Systems, and Star-Cloudlets. By R. A. Proctor, B. A. Crown 8vo. with numerous Illustrations. *Nearly ready.*

The Orbs Around Us; a Series of Familiar Essays on the Moon and Planets, Meteors and Comets, the Sun and Coloured Pairs of Suns. By R. A. Proctor, B.A. Crown 8vo. price 7s. Gd.

Other "Worlds than Ours; the Plurality of Worlds Studied under the Light of Recent Scientific Researches. By R. A. Proctor, B.A. Third Edition, revised and corrected; with 14 Illustrations. Crown 8vo. 10s. Gd.

Celestial Objects for Common Telescopes. By T. W. Werr, M.A. F.R.A.S. New Edition, revised, with Map of the Moon and Woodcuts. *the press.*

A General Dictionary of Geography, Descriptive, Physical, Statistical, and Historical; forming a complete Gazetteer of the World. By A. Keith Johnston, F.R.S.E. New Edition. 8vo. price 31s. Gd.

The Public Schools Atlas of Modern Geography. In Thirty-one Maps, exhibiting clearly the more important Physical Features of the Countries delineated, and Noting all the Chief Places of Historical, Commercial, and Social Interest. Edited, with an Introduction, by the Rev. G. Butler, M.A. Imperial quarto, price 3s. Gd. sewed; 5s. cloth.

A New Star Atlas, for the Library, the School, and the Observatory, in Twelve Circular Maps (with Two Index Plates). Intended as a Companion to ' Webb's Celestial Objects for Common Telescopes.' With a Letterpress Introduction on the Study of the Stars, illustrated by 9 Diagrams. By Richard A. Proctor, B. A. Hon. Sec. B.A.S. Crown 8vo. 5».

*Natural History* a Natural Philosophy for General Readers and Young Persons; a Course of Physics divested of Mathematical Formula; and expressed in the language of daily life. Translated from Ganot's *Cours de Physique,* by E. Atkinson, Ph.

D. F.C.S. Crown 8vo. with 404 Woodcuts, price 7s. *Gd.*

Mrs. Marcet's Conversations on
Natural Philosophy. Revised by the Author's Son', and augmented by Conversations on Spectrum Analysis and Solar Chemistry. With 3G Plates. Crown 8vo. price 7s. *Gd.*

Ganot's Elementary Treatise on
Physics, Experimental and Applied, for the use of Colleges and Schools. Translated and Edited with the Author's sanction by E. Atkinson, Ph.D. F.C.S. New Edition, revised and enlarged; with a Coloured Plate and 726 Woodcuts. Post 8vo. 15s.

Text-Books of Science, Mechanical and Physical. The following may now be had, price 3s. *Gd.* each:— 1. Goodbye's Mechanism. 2. Bi.oxam's Metals. 3. Miller's Inorganic Chemistry. 4. Griffin's Algebra and Trigonometry. 5. Watson's Plane and Solid Geometry. 6. Maxwell's Theory of Heat. 7. Mehrifiei.d's Technical Arithmetic and Mensuration. 8. Anderson's Strength of Materials. Dove's Law Of Storms, considered in connexion with the ordinary Movements of the Atmosphere. Translated by R. H. Scott, M.A. T.C.D. 8vo. 10s. 6d.

The Correlation of Physical
Forces. By W. R. Grove, Q.C. V.P. R.S. Fifth Edition, revised, and Augmented by a Discourse on Continuity. 8vo. 10s. *Gd.* The *Discourse,* separately, pries 2s. *Gd.*

Fragments of Science. By John
Tyndall, I.L.D. F.R.S. Third Edition. 8vo. price 14s.

Heat a Mode of Motion. By John
Tyndall, LL.D. F.R.S. Fourth Edition. Crown 8vo. with Woodcuts, price 10s. *Gd.*

Sound; a Course of Eight Lectures delivered at the Royal Institution of Great Britain. By John Tyndall, LL.D. F.R.S. New Edition, with Portrait and Woodcuts. Crown 8vo. 9s.

Ld *Popular Science.*
Researches on Diamagnetism
and Magne-Crystallic Action; including the Question of Diamagnetic Polarity. By
John Tyndall, LL.D. F.R.S. With 6 Plates and many Woodcuts. 8vo. 14s.

Notes of a Course of Nine Lectures on Light, delivered at the Royal Institution, A.d. 1869. By J. Tyndall, LL.D. F.R.S. Crown 8vo. Is. sewed, or Is. *Gd.* cloth.

Notes of a Course of Seven Lectures on Electrical Phenomena and Theories, delivered at the Royal Institution, A.d. 1870. By John Tyndall, LL.D. F.R.S. Crown 8vo. Is. sewed, or Is. *Gd.* cloth.

A Treatise on Electricity, in
Theory and Practice. By A. De La Rive, Prof, in the Academy of Geneva. Translated by C. V. Walker, F.R.S. 3 vols 8vo. with Woodcuts, £3. 13s.

Light Science for Leisure Hours; a Series of Familiar Essays on Scientific Subjects, Natural Phenomena, &c. By R. A. Proctor, B.A. Crown 8vo. price 7s. *Gd.*

Light: its Influence on Life and Health. By Forbes Winslow, M.D. D.C. L. Oxon. (Hon.) Fcp. 8vo. 6s.

Professor Owen's Lectures on the Comparative Anatomy and Physiology of the Invertebrate Animals. Second Edition, with 235 Woodcuts. 8vo. 21s.

The Comparative Anatomy and
Physiology of the Vertebrate Animals. By Richard Owen, F.R.S. D.C.L. With 1,472 Woodcuts. 3 vols. 8vo. £3 13s. *Gd.*

Kirby and Spence's Introduction to Entomology, or Elements of the Natural History of Insects. Crown 8vo. 5s.

Homes Without Hands; a Description of the Habitations of Animals, classed according to their Principle of Construction. By Rev. J. G. Wood, M.A. F.L.S. With about 140 Vignettes on Wood. 8vo. 21s.

Strange Dwellings; a Description of the Habitations of Animals, abridged from 'Homes without Hands.' By J. G. Wood, M.A. F.L.S. With a New Frontispiece and about 60 other Woodcut Illustrations. Crown 8vo. price 7s. *Gd.* 10 NEW WORKS Purlished

Ry LONGMANS And CO.
Van Der Hoeven's Handbook of
Zoology. Translated from the Second Dutch Edition by the Kev. W. Clark, M. D. F.R.S. 2 vols. 8vo. with 24 Plates of Figures, 60s.

The Harmonies of Nature and
Unity of Creation. By Dr. G. Hartwig. 8vo. with numerous Illustrations, 18s.

The Sea and its Living "Wonders. By the same Author. Third Edition, enlarged. 8vo. with many Illustrations, 21».

The Subterranean World. By the same Author. With 3 Maps and about 80 Woodcut Illustrations, including 8 full size of page. 8vo. price 21s.

The Polar World: a Popular Description of Man and Nature in the Arctic and Antarctic Regions of the Globe. By the same Author. With 8 Chromoxylographs, 3 Maps, and 85 Woodcuts. 8vo. 21s.

A Familiar History of Birds.
By E. Stanley, D.D. late Lord Bishop of Norwich. Fcp. with Woodcuts, 3s. 6f.

Insects at Home; a Popular Account of British Insects, their Structure, Habits, and Transformations. By the Rev. J. G. Wood, M.A. F.L.S. With upwards of 700 Illustrations engraved on Wood. 8vo. price 21s.

Insects Abroad; being a Popular Account of Foreign Insects, their Structure, Habits, and Transformations. By J. G. Wood, M.A. F.L.S. Author of 'Homes without Hands &c. In One Volume, printed and illustrated uniformly with 'Insects at Home,, to which it will form a Sequel and Companion. in *the press.*

The Primitive Inhabitants of
Scandinavia. Containing a Description of the Implements, Dwellings, Tombs, and Mode of Living of the Savages in the North of Europe during the Stone Age. By Sven Nilsson. 8vo. Plates and Woodcuts, 18s.

The Origin of Civilisation, and the Primitive Condition of Man; Mental and Social Condition of Savages. By Sir John Lurrock, Bart. M.P. F.R.S. Second Edition, with 25 Woodcuts. 8vo. 16s.

The Ancient Stone Implements,
Weapons, and Ornaments, of Great Britain. By John Evans, F.R.S. F.S.A. 8vo. with 2 Plates and 476 Woodcuts, price 28s.

Mankind, their Origin and Destiny. By an M.A. of Balliol College, Oxford.

Containing a New Translation of the First Three Chapters of Genesis; a Critical Examination of the First Two Gospels; an Explanation of the Apocalypse j and the Origin and Secret Meaning of the Mythological and Mystical Teaching of the Ancients. With 31 Illustrations. 8vo. price 31s. Gd.

An Exposition of Fallacies in the Hypothesis of Mr. Darwin. By C. R. Bree, M.D. F.Z.S. Author of' Birds of Europe not Observed in the British Isles' &c. With 36 Woodcuts. Crown 8vo. price 14s.

Bible Animals; a Description of every Living Creature mentioned in the Scriptures, from the Ape to the Coral. By the Rev. J. G. Wood, M.A. F.L.S. With about 100 Vignettes on Wood. 8vo. 21s.

Maunder's Treasury of Natural History, or Popular Dictionary of Zoology. Revised and corrected by T. S. Corrold, M.D. Fcp. 8vo. with 900 Woodcuts, 6s.

The Elements of Botany for Families and Schools. Tenth Edition, revised by Thomas Moore, F.L.S. Fcp. with 154 Woodcuts, 2s. Gd.

The Treasury of Botany, or Popular Dictionary of the Vegetable Kingdom; with which is incorporated a Glossary of Botanical Terms. Edited by J. Lindley, F.R.S. and T. Moore, F.L.S. Pp. 1,274, with 274 Woodcuts and 20 Steel Plates. Two Parts, fcp. 8vo. 12s.

The Rose Amateur's Guide. By Thomas Rivers. New Edition. Fcp. 4s.

Loudon'sEncyclopsedia of Plants; comprising the Specific Character, Description, Culture, History, &c. of all the Plants found in Great Britain. With upwards of 12,000 Woodcuts. 8vo. 42s.

Maunder's Scientific and Literary Treasury; a Popular Encyclopasdia of Science, Literature, and Art. New Edition, in part rewritten, with above 1,000 new articles, by J. Y. Johnson. Fcp. 6s.

A Dictionary of Science, Literature, and Art. Fourth Edition, re-edited by the late W. T. Brande (the Author) and George W. Cox, M.A. 3 vols, medium 8vo. price 63s. cloth.

NEW WORKS Purlished Rt LONGMANS And CO. 11 *Chemistry, Medicine, Surgery,* and *the Allied Sciences.*

A Dictionary of Chemistry and the Allied Branches of other Sciences. By Henry Watts, F.C.S. assisted by eminent Scientific and Practical Chemists. 5 vols, medium 8vo. price £7 3s.

Supplement, completing the Record of Discovery to the end of 186'J. 8vo. 31s. Gd.

Contributions to Molecular Physics in the domain of Radiant Heat j a Series of Memoirs published in the Philosophical Transactions, &c. By Joiln Tyndall, LL.D. F.R.S. With 2 Plates and 31 Woodcuts. 8vo. price l6s.

Elements of Chemistry, Theoretical and Practical. By William A. Miller, M. D. LL.D. Professor of Chemistry, King,s College, London. New Edition. 3 vols. 8vo. £3.

Part I. Chemical Physics, 15s.
Part II. Inorganic Chemistry, 21s.
Part III. Organic Chemistry, 24s.

A Course of Practical Chemistry, for the use of Medical Students. By W. Odlino.m.b.f.r.s. New Edition, with 70 new Woodcuts. Crown 8vo. 7s. Gd.

Outlines of Chemistry; or, Brief Notes of Chemical Facts. By the same Author. Crown 8vo. 7s. Gd.

A Manual of Chemical Physiology, including its Points of Contact with Pathology. By J. L. W. Thudicuum, M. D. 8vo. with Woodcuts, price 7s. Gd.

Select Methods in Chemical Analysis, chiefly Inorganic. By William Crookes, F.R.S. With 22 Woodcuts. Crown 8vo. price 12s. Gd.

Chemical Notes for the Lecture Room. By Thomas Wood, F.C.S. 2 vols, crown 8vo. I. on Heat, &c. price 5s. II. on the Metals, price 5s.

The Diagnosis, Pathology, and Treatment of Diseases of Women; including the Diagnosis of Pregnancy. By Graily Hewitt, M.D. &c. Third Edition, revised and for the most part re-writtcn; with 132 Woodcuts. 8vo. 24s.

Lectures on the Diseases of Infancy and Childhood. By Charles West, M.D. &c. Fifth Edition. 8vo. 16s.

On Some Disorders of the Nervous System in Childhood. Being the Lumleian Lectures delivered before the Royal College of Physicians in March 1871. By Charles West, M.D. Crown 8vo, 5s.

On the Surgical Treatment of Children's Diseases. By T. Holmes, M.A. &c. late Surgeon to the Hospital for Sick Children. Second Edition, with 9 Plates and 112 Woodcuts. 8vo. 21»".

Lectures on the Principles and Practice of Physic. By Sir Thomas WatSon, Bart. M.D. Physician-in-Ordinary to the Queen. Fifth Edition, thoroughly revised. 2 vols. 8vo. price 36s.

Lectures on Surgical Pathology. By Sir James Paget, Bart F.R.S. Third Edition, revised and re-edited by the Author and Professor W. Turner, M.B. 8vo. with 131 Woodcuts, 21s.

Cooper's Dictionary of Practical Surgery and Encyclopaedia of Surgical Science. New Edition, brought down to the present time. By S. A. Lane, Surgeon to St. Mary,s Hospital, &c. assisted by various Eminent Surgeons. 2 vols. 8vo. price 25s. each.

Pulmonary Consumption; its Nature, Varieties, and Treatment: with an Analysis of One Thousand Cases to exemplify its Duration. By C. J. B. Williams, M.D. F.R.S. and C T. Williams, M.A. M.D. Oxon. Post 8vo. price 10s. Gd.

Anatomy, Descriptive and Surgical. By Henry Gray, F.R.S. With about 410 Woodcuts from Dissections. Sixth Edition, by T. Holmes, M.A. Cantab. With a New Introduction by the Editor. Royal 8vo. 28s.

The House I Live in; or,Popular Illustrations of the Structure and Functions of the Human Body. Edited by T. G. Girtin. New Edition, with 25 Woodcuts. 16mo. price 2s. Gd.

The Science and Art of Surgery; being a Treatise on Surgical Injuries, Diseases, and Operations. By John Eric Erichsen, Senior Surgeon to University College Hospital, and Holme Professor of Clinical Surgery in University College, London. A New Edition, being the Sixth, revised and enlarged; with 712 Woodcuts. 2 vols. 8vo. price 32s.

A System of Surgery, Theoretical and Practical, in Treatises by Various

Authors. Edited by T. Holmes, M.A. &c. Surgeon and Lecturer on Surgery at St. George,s Hospital, and Surgeon-in-Chief to the Metropolitan Police. Second Edition, thoroughly revised, with numerous Illustrations. 5 vols. 8vo. £5 5s.

12 NEW WORKS Published Ry LONGMANS And CO.

Clinical Lectures on Diseases of the Liver, Jaundice, and Abdominal Dropsy. By C. Murchison, M.D. Physician to the Middlesex Hospital. Post 8vo. with 25 Woodcuts, 10s. Gd.

Todd and Bowman's Physiological Anatomy and Physiology of Man. With numerous Illustrations. Vol. II. 8vo. price 25».

Vol. I. New Edition by Dr. Lionel S. Beale, F.R.S. in course of publication, with numerous Illustrations. Parts I. and II. price 7s. Gd. each.

Outlines of Physiology, Human and Comparative. By Jons Marsha Ll, F.R.C.S. Surgeon to the University College Hospital. 2 vols, crown 8vo. with 122 Woodcuts, 32s.

Copland's Dictionary of Practical Medicine, abridged from the larger work, and throughout brought down to the present state of Medical Science. 8vo. 36s.

Dr. Pereira's Elements of Materia Medica and Therapeutics, abridged and adapted for the use of Medical and Pharmaceutical Practitioners and Students. Edited by Professor Bentley, F.L.S. 4c. and by Dr. Redwood, F.C.S. &c. With 125 Woodcut Illustrations. 8vo. price 25s.

The Essentials of Materia Medica and Therapeutics. By Alfred Baring Garrod, M.D. F.R.S". &c Physician to King,s College Hospital. Third Edition, Sixth Impression, brought up to 1870. Crown 8vo. price 12s. Gd. The Fine Arts, and Grotesque Animals, invented, described, and portrayed by E. W. Cooke, R.A., F.R.S. in Twenty-Four Plates, with Elucidatory Comments. Roval 4to. price 21s.

In Fairyland; Pictures from the ElfWorld. By Richard Doyle. With a Poem by W. Allingham. With Sixteen Plates, containing Thirty-six Designs printed in Colours. Folio, 31s. Gd.

Albert Durer, his Life and Works; including Autobiographical Papers and Complete Catalogues. By William B. Scott. With Six Etchings by the Author and other Illustrations. 8vo. 16s.

Half-Hour Lectures on the History and Practice of the Fine and Ornamental Arts. By. W. B. Scott. Second Edition. Crown 8vo. with 50 Woodcut Illustrations, 8s. Gd.

The Chorale Book for England: the Hymns Translated by Miss C. WinkWorth; the Tunes arranged by Prof. W. S. Bennett and Otto Goldschmidt. Fcp. 4to. 12s. Gd. The New Testament, illustrated with

Wood Engravings after the Early Masters, chiefly of the Italian School. Crown 4to. 63s. cloth, gilt top; or £5 5s. morocco.

The Life of Man Symbolised by the Months of the Year in their Seasons and Phases. Text selected by Richard Pigot. 25 Illustrations on Wood from Original Designs by John Leighton, F.S.A. Quarto, 42s.

*Illustrated Editions.*

Cats and Farlie's Moral Emblems; with Aphorisms, Adages, and Proverbs of all Nations: comprising 121 Illustrations on Wood by J. Leighton, F.S.A. with an appropriate Text by R. Pigot. Imperial 8vo. 31s. Gd.

Sacred and Legendary Art. By Mrs. Jameson. 6 vols, square crown 8vo. price £5 15s. Gd. as follows:—

Legends of the Saints and Martyrs. New Edition, with 19 Etchings and 187 Woodcuts. 2 vols, price 31s. Gd.

Legends of the Monastic Orders. New Edition, with 11 Etchings and 88 Woodcuts. 1 vol. price 21s.

Legends of the Madonna. New'Edition, with 27 Etchings and 165 Woodcuts. 1 vol. price 21s.

The History of Our Lord, with that of H is Types and Precursors. Completed by Lady Eastlake. Revised Edition, with 13 Etchings and 281 Woodcuts. 2 vols, price 42s.

Lyra Germanica, the Christian Year. Translated by Catherine Winkworth, with 125 Illustrations on Wood drawn by J. Leighton, F.S.A. Quarto, 21s.

Lyra Germanica. the Christian Lift. Translated by Catherine Winkworth; with about 200 Woodcut Illustrations by J. Leighton, F.S.A. and other Artists. Quarto, 21s.

NEW WORKS Purlished Ry LONGMANS And CO. 18 *The Useful Arts, Manufactures, $c.*

Gwilt's Encyclopaedia of Architecture, with above 1,600 Woodcuts. Fifth Edition, with Alterations and considerable Additions, by Wyatt Papworth. 8vo. price 52s. Gd.

A Manual of Architecture: being a Concise History and Explanation of the principal Styles of European Architecture, Ancient, Mediaeval, and Renaissance; with their Chief Variations and a Glossary of Technical Terms. By Thomas Mitchell. With 150 Woodcuts. Crown 8vo. 10s. 6f.

History of the Gothic Revival; an Attempt to shew how far the laste for Mediasval Architecture was retained in England during the last two centuries, and has been re-developed in the present. By C. L. Eastlake, Architect. With 48 Illustrations (36 full size of page). Imperial 8vo. price 31s. Gd.

Hints on Household Taste in Furniture, Upholstery, and other Details. By Charles L. Eastlake, Architect. New Edition, with about 90 Illustrations. Square crown 8vo. 18s.

Lathes and Turning, Simple, Mechanical, and Ornamental. By W. Henry Northcott. With about 240 Illustrations on Steel and Wood. 8vo. 18s.

Perspective; or, the Art of Drawing what one Sees. Explained and adapted to the use of those Sketching from Nature. By Lieut, W. H. Collins, R.E. F.R.A.S. With 37 Woodcuts. Crown 8vo. price 5s.

Principles of Mechanism, designed for the use of Students in the Universities, and for Engineering Students generally. By R. Willis, M.A. F.R.S. &c. Jacksonian Professor in the Univ. of Cambridge. Second Edition; with 374 Woodcuts. 8vo. 18s.

Handbook of Practical Telegraphy.

By R. S. Culley, Memb. Inst. C.E. Engineer-in-Chief of Telegraphs to the Poet-Office. Fifth Edition, revised and enlarged; with 118 Woodcuts and 9 Plates. 8vo. price 14s.

Ure's Dictionary of Arts, Manufactures, and Mines. Sixth Edition, rewritten and greatly enlarged by Rorert Hdkt, F.R.S. assisted by numerous Contributors. With 2,000 Woodcuts. 3 vols, medium 8vo. £4 lis. Gd.

Encyclopsedia of Civil Engineering, Historical, Theoretical, and Practical. By E. Cresy, C.E. With above 3,000 Woodcuts. 8vo. 42s.

Catechism of the Steam Engine, in its various Applications to Mines, Mills, Steam Navigation, Railways, and Agriculture. By John Bourne, C.E. NewEdition, with 89 Woodcuts. Fcp. 8vo. 6s.

Handbook of the Steam Engine. By John Bourne, C.E. forming a Key to the Author's Catechism of the Steam Engine. With 67 Woodcuts. Fcp. 8vo. price 9s.

Recent Improvements in the Steam-Engine. By John Bourne, C.E. New Edition, including many New Examples, with 124 Woodcuts. Fcp. 8vo. 6s.

A Treatise on the Steam Engine, in its various Applications to Mines, Mills, Steam Navigation, Railways, and Agriculture. By J. Bourne, C.E. New Edition; with Portrait, 37 Plates, and 546 Woodcuts. 4to. 42s.

A Treatise on the Screw Propeller, Screw Vessels, and Screw Engines, as adapted for purposes of Peace and War. By John Bourne, C.E. Third Edition, with 54 Plates and 287 Woodcuts. Quarto, price 63s.

Bourne's Examples of Modern Steam, Air, and Gas Engines of the most Approved Types, as employed for Pumping, for Driving Machinery, for Locomotion, and for Agriculture, minutely and practically described. In course of publication, to be completed in Twenty-four Parts, price 2s. Gd. each, forming One Volume, with about 50 Plates and 400 Woodcuts.

Treatise on Mills and Millwork. By Sir W. Fairrairn, Bart. F.R.S. New Edition, with 18 Plates and 322 Woodcuts. 2 vols. 8vo. 32s.

Useful Information for Engineers. By the same Author. First, Second, and Third Series, with many Plates and Woodcuts. 3 vols, crown 8vo. 10s. Gd. each.

The Application of Cast and Wrought Iron to Building Purposes. By the same Author. Fourth Edition, with 6 Plates and 118 Woodcuts. 8vo. 16s.

Iron Ship Building, its History and Progress, as comprised in a Series of Experimental Researches. By Sir W. FairRairn, Bart. F.R.S. With 4 Plates and 130 Woodcuts, 8vo. 18s.

The Strains in Trusses Computed by means of Diagrams; with 20 Examples drawn to Scale. By F. A. Ranken, M. A. C.E. Lecturer at the Hartley Institution, Southampton. With 35 Diagrams. Square crown 8vo. price 6s. 6d.

14 NEW WORKS Purlished Ry LONGMANS And CO.

Mitchell's Manual of Practical Assaying. Third Edition for the most part re-written, with all the recent Discoveries incorporated. By W. Crookes, F.R.S. With 188 Woodcuts. 8vo. 28s.

The Art of Perfumery; the History and Theory of Odours, and the Methods of Extracting the Aromas of Plants. By Dr. Piesse, F.C.S. Third Edition, with 53 Woodcuts. Crown 8vo. 10s. Gd.

Bayldon's Art of Valuing Rents and Tillages, and Claims of Tenants upon Quitting Farms, both at Michaelmas and Lady-Day. Eighth Edition, revised by J. C. Morton. 8vo. 10s. Gd.

On the Manufacture of BeetBoot Sugar in England and Ireland. By William Crookes, F.R.S. With 11 Woodcuts. 8vo. 8s. Gd.

Practical Treatise on Metallurgy, adapted from the last German Edition of Professor Kerl's *Metallurgy* by W. Crookes, F.R.S. &c. and E. Rohrig, Ph. D. M.E. 3 vols. 8vo. with 625 Woodcuts, price SA 19s.

Loudon's Encyclopaedia of Agriculture: comprising the Laying-out, Improvement, and Management of Landed Property, and the Cultivation and Economy of the Productions of Agriculture. With 1,100 Woodcuts. 8vo. 21s.

Loudon's Encyclopaedia of Gardening. comprising the Theory and Practice of Horticulture, Floriculture, Arboriculture, and Landscape Gardening. With 1,000 Woodcuts. 8vo. 21s. *Religious* and *Moral Works*.

The Outlines of the Christian Ministry Delineated, and brought to the Test of Reason, Holy Scripture, History, and Experience, with a view to the Reconciliation of Existing Differences concerning it, especially between Presbyterians and Episcopalians. By Christopher WordsWorth, D.C.L. &c. Bishop of St. Andrew's, and Fellow of Winchester College. Crown 8vo. price 7s. Gd.

Christian Counsels, selected from the Devotional Works; of Fenelon, Archbishop of Cambrai. Translated by A. M. James. Crown 8vo. price 5s.

Ecclesiastical Beform. Nine Essays by various Writers. Edited by the Rev. Orry Shipley, M.A. Crown 8vo. *Nearly ready.*

Authority and Conscience; a Free Debate on the Tendency of Dogmatic Theology and on the Characteristics of Faith. Edited by Conway Morel. Post 8vo. 7s. 6Z.

Reasons of Paith; or, the Order of the Christian Argument Developed and Explained. By the Rev. G. S. Drew, M.A. Second Edition, revised and enlarged. Fcp.
5 8vo. 6s.

Christ the Consoler; a Book of Comfort for the Sick. With a Preface by the Right Rev. the Lord Bishop of Carlisle. Small 8vo. 6s.

The True Doctrine of the Eucharist. By Thomas S. L. Vogan, D.D. Canon'and Prebendary of Chichester and Rural Dean. 8vo. 18s.

The Student's Compendium of the Book of Common Prayer; being Notes Historical and Explanatory of the Liturgy of the Church of England. By the Rev. H. Allden Nash. Fcp. 8vo. price 2s. Sd.

Synonyms of the Old Testament, their Bearing on Christian Faith and Practice. By the Rev. Rorert B. GirdleStone, M.A. 8vo. price 15s.

Fundamentals; or, Bases of Belief

concerning Man and God: a Handbook of Mental, Moral, and Religious Philosophy. By the Rev. T. Griffith, M.A. 8vo. price 10s. *Gd.*

An Introduction to the Theology of the Church of England, in an Exposition of the Thirty-nine Articles. By the Bev. T. P. Boultree, LL.D. Fcp. 8vo. price 6s.

Christian Sacerdotalism, viewed from a Layman's standpoint or tried by Holy Scripture and the Early Fathers; with a short Sketch of the State of the Church from the end of the Third to the Reformation in the beginning of the Sixteenth Century. By John Jardine, M. A. LL.D. 8vo. 8s. *Gd.*

Prayers for the Family and for Private Use, selected from the Collection of the late Baron Bunsen, and Translated by Catherine Wiwkwoeth. Fcp. 8vo. price 3s. *Gd.*

Churches and their Creeds. By the Rev. Sir Philip Peering, Bart, late Scholar of Trin. Coll. Cambridge, and University Medallist. Crown 8vo. 10s. *Gd.* NEW WORKS Published Ey LONGMANS And CO.

IS

The Truth of the Bible; Evidence from the Mosaic and other Records of Creation; the Origin and Antiquity of Man; the Science of Scripture; and from the Arclueology of Different Nations of the Earth. By the Rev. B. W. Savile, M. A. Crown 8vo. 7s. *Gd.*

Considerations on the Revision of the English New Testament. By C. J. Ellicott, D.D. Lord Bishop of Gloucester and Bristol. Post 8vo. price 5s. *Gd.*

An Exposition of the 39 Articles, Historical and Doctrinal. By E. Harold
Browne, D.D. Lord Bishop of Ely. Ninth
Edition. 8vo. 16s.

The Voyage and Shipwreck of St. Paul; with Dissertations on the Ships and Navigation of the Ancients. By James Smith, F.R.S. Crown 8vo. Charts, 10s. *Gd.*

The Life and Epistles of St. Paul. By the Rev. W. J. Conybeare, M.A. and the Very Rev. J. S. Howson, D.D. Dean of Chester. Three Editions:—

Library Edition, with all the Original Illustrations, Maps, Landscapes on Steel,
Woodcuts, &c. 2 vols. 4to. 48s.

Intermedlvte Edition, with a Selection of Maps, Plates, and Woodcuts. 2 vols, square crown 8vo. 21s.

Student's Edition, revised and condensed, with 46 Illustrations and Maps. 1 vol. crown 8vo. 9s.

Evidence of the Truth of the
Christian Religion derived from the Literal Fulfilment of Prophecy. By Alexander Keith, D.D. 37th Edition, with numerous Plates, in square 8vo. 12s. *Gd.;* also the 39th Edition, in post 8vo. with 5 Plates, 6s. The History and Destiny of the World and of the Church, according to Scripture. By the same Author. Square 8vo. with 40 Illustrations, 10s.

The History and Literature of the Israelites, according to the Old Testament and the Apocrypha. By C. De Rothschild and A. De Rothschild. Second Edition. 2 vols, crown 8vo. 12s. *Gd.* Abridged Edition, in 1 vol. fcp. 8vo. 3s. *Gd.*

Ewald's History of Israel to the Death of Moses. Translated from the German. Edited, with a Preface and an Appendix, by Russell Martineau, M.A. Second Edition. 2 vols. 8vo. 24s. Vols. III. and IV. edited by J. E. Carpenter, M. A. price,,21s.

England and Christendom. By Archbishop Manning, D.D. Post 8vo. price 10s *Gd.*

The Pontificate of Pius the Ninth; being the Third Edition, enlarged and continued, of 'Rome and its Ruler.' By J. F. Maguire, M.P. Post 8vo. Portrait, price 12s. Gd.

Ignatius Loyola and the Early Jesuits. By Stewart Rose New Edition, revised. 8vo. with Portrait, 16s.

An Introduction to the Study of the New Testament, Critical, Exegetical, and Theological. By the Rev. S. Davidson, D.D. LL.D. 2 vols. 8vo. 30s.

A Critical and Grammatical Commentary on St. Paul's Epistles. By C. J. Ellicott, D.D. Lord Bishop of Gloucester and Bristol. 8vo.

Galatians, Fourth Edition, 8s. *Gd*

Ephesians, Fourth Edition, 8s. *Sd.*
Pastoral Epistles, Fourth Edition, 10s. 6d.
Philippians, Colossians, and Philemon, Third Edition, 10s. *Gd.*
Thessalonians, Third Edition, 7s. *Gd.*
Historical Lectures on the Life of Our Lord Jesus Christ: being the Hulsean
Lectures for 1859. By C. J. Ellicott, D. D.
Fifth Edition. 8vo. 12s.

TheGreek Testament; with Motes, Grammatical and Exegetical. By the Rev.
W. Webster, M.A. and the Rev. W. F. Wilkinson, M.A. 2 vols. 8vo. £2. 4s.

Home's Introduction to the Critical Study and Knowledge of the Holy Scriptures. Twelfth Edition; with 4 Maps and 22 Woodcuts. 4 vols. 8vo. 42s.

The Treasury of Bible Knowledge; being a Dictionary of the Books, Persons, Places, Events, and other Matters of which mention is made in Holy Scripture. By Rev. J. Ayre, MA. With Maps, 15 Plates, and numerous Woodcuts. Fcp. 8vo. price 6s.

Every-day Scripture Difficulties explained and illustrated. By J. E. PrescoTt, M.A. I. *Matthew* and *Mark*; II. *Luke* and *John*. 2 vols. 8vo. price 9s. each.

The Pentateuch and Book of Joshua Critically Examined. By the Right Rev. J. W. Colenso, D.D. Lord Bishop of Natal. Crown 8vo. price 6s. Part V. Genesis Analysed and Separated, and the Ages of its Writers determined 8vo. 18s.

Part VI. The Later Legislation of the Pentateuch. 8vo. 24s.

The Formation of Christendom. By T. W. Allies. Parts I. and II. 3vo. price 12s. each.

16 NEW WORKS Published By LONGMANS And CO.

Pour Discourses of Chrysostom, chiefly on the parable of the Rich Man and Lazarus. Translated by F. Allen, B.A. Crown 8vo. *3t.* 6d.

Thoughts for the Age. By Elizabeth M. Sewell, Author of Amy Herbert. New Edition. Fcp. 8vo. price 5s.

Passing Thoughts on Eeligion. By the same Author. Fcp. 3«. Gd.

Self-examination before Confirmation. By the same Author. 32mo. Is. Gd.

Thoughts for the Holy "Week, for Young Persons. By the same Author. New Edition. Fcp. 8vo. 2s.

Headings for a Month Preparatory to Confirmation from Writers of the Early and English Church. By the same. Fcp. 4s.

Headings for Every Day in Lent, compiled from the Writings of Bishop Jeremy Taylor. By the same Author. Fcp. 5s.

Preparation for the Holy Communion; the Devotions chiefly from the works of Jeremy Taylor. By the same. 32mo. 3s.

Bishop Jeremy Taylor's Entire Works; with Life by Bishop Heber. Revised and corrected by the Rev. C. P Eden. 10 vols. £5. 5».

Spiritual Songs' for the Sundays and Holidays throughout the Year. By J. S. B. Monsell, LL.D. Vicar of Egham and Rural Dean. Fourth Edition, Sixth Thousand. Fcp. price 4s. Gd.

The Beatitudes. By the same Author. Third Edition, revised. Fcp. 3s. Gd.

His Presence not his Memory, 1855. By the same Author, in memory of his Son. Sixth Edition. 16mo. Is.

Lyra Germanica, translated from the German by Miss C. Winkworth. First Series, the *Christian Year,* Hymns for the Sundays and Chief Festivals of the Church; Second Series, the *Christian Life.* Fcp. 8vo. price 3s. Gd. each Series.

Endeavours after the Christian Life; Discourses. By James Martineau. Fourth Edition. Post 8vo. price 7s. 6d.

*Travels, Voyages, §c.*

Six Months in California. By J. G. Player-frowd. Post 8vo. price Gs.

The Japanese in America. By Charles;lanman, American Secretary, Japanese Legation, Washington, U.S.A. Post 8vo. price 10s. Gd.

My Wife and I in Queensland; Eight Years' Experience in the Colony, with some account of Polynesian Labour. By Charles H. Eden. With Map and Frontispiece. Crown 8vo. price 9s.

Life in India; a Series of Sketches shewing something of the Anglo-Indian, the Land he lives in, and the People among whom he lives. By Edward Braddon. Post 8vo. price 9s.

How to See Norway. By Captain J.r.campbell. With Map and 5 Woodcuts. Fcp. 8vo. price 5s.

Pau and the Pyrenees. By Count Henry Russell, Member of the Alpine Club. With 2 Maps. Fcp. 8vo. price 5s.

Hours of Exercise in the Alps. By John Tyndall, LL.D., F.R S. Second Edition, with Seven Woodcuts by E. Whymper. Crown 8vo. price 12s. Gd.

Westward by Bail; the New Route to the East. By W.f.rae. Second Edition. Post 8vo. with Map, price 10s. 6d.

Travels in the Central Caucasus and Bashan, including Visits to Ararat and Tabreez and Ascents of Kazbek and Elbruz. By Douglas W. Fueshfield. Square crown 8vo. with Maps, &c., 18s.

Cadore or Titian's Country. By Josiah Gilbert, one of the Authors of the Dolomite Mountains/ With Map, Facsimile, and 48 Illustrations. Imp. 8vo. 31s. 6d.

The Playground of Europe. By Leslie Stephen, late President of the Alpine Club. With 4 Illustrations on Wood by E. Whymper. Crown 8vo. 10s. 6d.

Zigzagging amongst Dolomites; with more than 300 Illustrations by the Author. By the Author of' How we Spent the Summer.' Oblong 4to. price 15s.

The Dolomite Mountains. Excursions through Tyrol, Carinthia, Carniola, and Friuli. By J. Gilbert and G. C. Churchill, F.R.G.S. With numerous Illustrations. Square crown 8vo. 21s.

How we Spent the Summer; or, a Voyage en Zigzag in Switzerland;'and Tyrol with some Members of the Alpine Club. Third Edition, re-drawn. In oblong 4to. with about 300 Illustrations, 15s. Pictures in Tyrol and Elsewhere. From a Family Sketch-Book. By the same Author. Second Edition. 4to. with many Illustrations, 21s.

NEW WORKS Purlished Ry LONGMANS And CO. 17

Beaten Tracks; or, Pen and Pencil Sketches in Italy. By the Author of' How we spent the Summer., With 42 Plates of Sketches. 8vo. 16s.

The Alpine Club Map of the Chain of Mont Blanc, from an actual Survey in 18(13— 1864. By A. Adams-eeilly, F.R.G.S. M.A.C. In Chromolithography on extra stout drawing paper 28in. x 17in. price 10s. or mounted on canvas in a folding case, 12s. Gd.

History of Discovery in our Australasian Colonies, Australia, Tasmania, and New Zealand, from the Earliest Date to the Present Day. By William Howitt. 2 vols. 8vo. with 3 Maps, 20s.

Visits to Kemarkable Places: Old Halls, Battle-Fields, and Scenes illustrative of striking Passages in English History and Poetry. By the same Author. 2 vols, square crown 8vo. with Wood Engravings, 25s.

Guide to the Pyrenees, for the use of Mountaineers. By Charles Packe. Second Edition, with Maps, &c. anJ Appendix. Crown 8vo. 7s. Gd.

The Alpine Guide. By John Ball M.R.I.A. late President of the Alpine Club.

Post 8vo. with Maps and other Illustrations. Guide to the Eastern Alps, price lus.Ctf. Guide to the Western Alps, including Mont Blanc, Monte Rosa, Zermatt, &c. price 6s. 6c/.

Guide to the Central Alps, including all the Oberland District, price 7s. Gd.

Introduction on Alpine Travelling in general, and on the Geology of the Alps, price 1s. Either of the Three Volumes or Parts of the *Alpine Guide* maybe had with this Introduction prefixed, price 1s. extra.

The Eural Life of England. By William Howitt. Woodcuts by Bewick and Williams. Medium 8vo. 12s. *Gd.* Works *of Fiction.*

Yarndale; a Story of Lancashire Life. By a Lancashire Man. 3 vols, post 8vo. price 21s.

The Burgomaster's Family; or, Weal and Woe in a Little World. By

Christine M,uller. Translated from the Dutch by Sir J. G. Silvw Lefevre, K.C. B,

F.B.S. Crown 8vo. price Gs.

Popular Romances of the Middle Ages. By the Rev. Gkorge W..Cox, M.A.

Author of 'The Mythology of the Aryan Nations &c. and Eustace Hinton Jones. Crown 8vo. 10s. Gd.

Tales of the Teutonic Lands; a Sequel to ' Popular Romances of the Middle

Ages., By George W. Cox, M.A. late Scholar of Trinity College, Oxford; and Eustace Hinton Jones. Crown 8vo. price 10s. Gd.

Hartland Forest; a Legend of North Devon. By Mrs. Bray, Author of 'The White Hoods,, 'Life of Stothard,, &c. Post 8vo. with Frontispiece, 4s. Gd.

Novels and Tales. By the Right Hon. Benjamin Disraeli, M.P. Cabinet Editions, complete in Ten Volumes, crown 8vo. price 6s. each, as follows:—
Lothair, 6s. I Venetia, 6s.

Coningsry, 6s. Alroy, Ixion, &c. 6s.
Sybil, 6s. Young Duke, &c. 6s.
Takcred, 6s. I Vivian Grey, 6s.
Contarini Flemixg, Ac. 6s.

Henrietta Temple, 6s.

18 NEW WORKS Published By LONGMANS And CO.

The Modern Novelist's Library.

Each Work, in crown 8vo. complete in a

Single Volume:— Melville's Digby Grand, 2s. boards; 2s. Gd. cloth. Gladiators, 2s. boards j 2s. Gd. cloth.

Good For Nothing, 2s. boards j 2s. Gd. cloth. Holmuy House, 2s. boards; 2s. Gd. cloth. 'Interpreter, 2s. boards; 2s. Gd. cloth.

— Kate Coventry, 2s. boards; 2s. Gd. cloth, i Queen's Maries, 2s. boards j 2s. Gd. cloth. Poetry and Ballads and Lyrics of Old Prance; with other Poems. By A. Lang, Fellow of Merton College, Oxford. Square fcp. 8vo. price 5s.

Thomas Moore's Poetical Works, with the Author's last Copyright Additions:—

Shamrock Edition, price 3s. Gd.
People's Edition, square cr. 8vo. 10s. Gd.

Library Edition, Portrait & Vignette, 14s.

Moore's Lalla Bookh, Tenniel's Edition, with 68 Wood Engravings from Original Drawings and other Illustrations. Fcp. 4to. 21s.

Moore's Irish Melodies, Maclise's Edition, with 161 Steel Plates from Original Drawings. Super-royal 8vo. 31s. Gd.

Miniature Edition of Moore's Irish Melodies, with Maclise's Illustrations (as above), reduced in Lithography. Imp. 16mo. 10s. Gd.

Lays of Ancient Borne; with Ivry and the Armada. By the Right Hon. Lord Macaulay. 16mo. 3s. Gd.

Lord Macaulay's Lays of Ancient Rorne. With 90 Illustrations on Wood, Original and from the Antique, from Drawings by G. Schabf. Fcp. 4to. 21s.

Miniature Edition of Lord Macaulay's

Lays of Ancient Rome, with Scharfs Illustrations (as above) reduced in Lithography. Imp. 16mo. 10». Gd.

Trollope's Warden Is. Gd. boards; 2» cloth.

BarchesterTowers,2s.boards; 2s. Gd. cloth.

Bramley-moore's Six Sisters Of The Valleys, 2s. boards; 2s. Gd. cloth.

Becker's Gallus; or, Roman Scenes of the Time of Augustus. Post 8vo. 7s. Gd.

Becker's Charicles: Illustrative of Private Life of the Ancient Greeks. Post 8vo. 7s. Gd.

Tales of Ancient Greece. By the Rev. G. W. Cox, M.A. late Scholar of Trin. Coll. Oxford. Crown 8vo. price 6s. Gd.

The Drama.

Southey's Poetical Works, with
. the Author's last Corrections and copyright Additions. Library Edition. Medium 8vo. with Portrait and Vignette, 14s.

Goldsmith's Poetical Works, Illustrated with Wood Engravings from Designs by Members of the Etching Club. Imp. 16mo. 7s. Gd.

Poems. By Jean Ingelow. Fifteenth Edition. Fcp. 8vo. 5s.

Poems by Jean Ingelow. With nearly 100 Illustrations by Eminent Artists, engraved on Wood by Dalzdzl Brothers. Fcp. 4to. 21s. A Story of Doom, and other Poems. By Jean Ingelow. Third Edition. Fcp. price 5s.

Bowdler's Family Shakspeare, cheaper Genuine Edition, complete in 1 vol. large type, with 36 Woodcut Illustrations, price lis. or in 6 pocket vols. 3s. Gd. each.

Horatii Opera, Library Edition, with Copious English Notes, Marginal References and Various Readings. Edited by the Rev. J. E. Tonge, M.A. 8vo. 21s.

The Odes and Epodes of Horace; a Metrical Translation into English, with Introduction and Commentaries. By Lord Lytton. With Latin Text. New Edition. Post 8vo. price 10s. Gd. The iEneid of Virgil Translated into English Verse. By John Coiongton, M.A. Corpus Professor of Latin in the University of Oxford. New Edition. Crown 8vo. 9s.

NEW WORKS Purlished Ry LONGMANS And CO. 19 Rural A!

Encyclopaedia of Rural Sports; a Complete Account, Historical, Practical, and Descriptive, of Hunting, Shooting, Fishing, Racing, &c. By D. P. Blaine. With above 600 Woodcuts (20 from Designs by John Leech). 8vo. 21s.

The Dead Shot, or Sportsman's Complete Guide; a Treatise on the Use of the Gun, Dog-breaking, Pigeon-shooting, &c. By Marksman. Fcp. with Plates, 5s.

A Book On Angling: being a Complete Treatise on the Art of Angling in every branch, including full Illustrated Lists of Salmon Flies. By Francis Francis. New Edition, with Portrait and 15 other Plates, plain and coloured. Post 8vo. 15s.

Wilcocks's Sea-Fisherman: comprising the Chief Methods of Hook and Line Fishing in the British and other Seas, a glance at Nets, and remarks on Boats and Boating. Second Edition, enlarged, with 80 Woodcuts. Post 8vo. 12s. Gd.

The Ply-Fisher's Entomology.

By Alfred Ronalds. With coloured Representations of the Natural and Artificial Insect. Sixth Edition, with 20 coloured Plates. 8vo. 14s.

The Ox, his Diseases and their Treatment; with an Essay on Parturition in the Cow. By J. R. Dorson, M.R.C.V.S. Crown 8vo. with Illustrations, 7s. Gd.

A Treatise on Horse-shoeing and Lameness. By Joseph Gamgee, Veterinary Surgeon, formerly Lecturer on the Principles and Practice of Farriery in the New Veterinary College, Edinburgh. 8vo. with 55 Woodcuts, 15s. *oris fyc.*

Blaine's Veterinary Art: a Treatise on the Anatomy, Physiology, and Curative Treatment of the Diseases of the Horse, Neat Cattle, and Sheep. Seventh Edition, revised and enlarged by C. Steel. 8vo. with Plates and Woodcuts, 18s.

Touatt on the Horse. Revised and enlarged by W. Watson, M.R.C.V.S. 8vo. with numerous Woodcuts, 12s. Gd.

Youatt on the Dog. (By the same Author.) 8vo. with numerous Woodcuts, 6s.

The Dog in Health and Disease. By Stonehenqe. With 73 Wood Engravings. New Edition, revised. Square crown 8vo. price 7s. Gd.

The Greyhound. By the same Author. Revised Edition, with 24 Portraits of Greyhounds. Square crown 8vo. 10s. Gd

The Setter; with Notices of the most Eminent Breeds now extant, Instructions how to Breed, Rear, and Break; Dog Shows, Field Trials, and General Management, Src. By Edward Laverack. With Two Portraits of Setters in Chromolithography. Crown 4to. price 7s. Gd.

Horses and Stables. By Colonel F. Fitzwygram, XV. the King,s Hussars. With 24 Plates of Woodcut Illustrations, containing very numerous Figures. 8vo. 15s.

The Horse's Foot, and how to keep it Sound. By W. Miles, Esq. Ninth Edition, with Illustrations. Imp. 8vo. 12s. Gd.

A Plain Treatise on Horse-shoeing. By the same Author. Sixth Edition, post 8vo. with Illustrations, 2s. Gd.

Stables and Stable Fittings. By the same. Imp. 8vo. with 13 Plates, 15s.

Remarks on Horses' Teeth, addressed to Purchasers. By the same. Post 8vo. 1s. Gd. *Works of Utility* and Modern Cookery for Private

Families, reduced to a System of Easy Practice in a Series of carefully-tested Receipts. By Eliza Acton. Newly revised and enlarged; with 8 Plates, Figures, and 150 Woodcuts. Fcp. 6s.

Maunder's Treasury of Knowledge and Library of Reference: comprising an English Dictionary and Grammar, Universal Gazetteer, Classical Dictionary, Chronology, Law Dictionary, Synopsis of the Peerage, Useful Tables, Ac. Fcp. 8vo. 6s.

Collieries and Colliers: a Handbook of the Law and Leading Cases relating thereto. By J. C. Fowler, Barrister. Second Edition. Fcp. 8vo. 7s. Gd. *General Information.*

The Theory and Practice of Banking. By Henry Dunning Macleod, M.A. Barrister-at-Law. Second Edition, entirely remodelled. 2 vols. 8vo. 30s.

M'Culloch's Dictionary, Practical, Theoretical, and Historical, of Commerce and Commercial Navigation. New Edition, revised throughout and corrected to the Present Time; with a Biographical Notice of the Author. Edited by H. G. Retd, Secretary to Mr. M'Culloch for many years. 8vo. price 6Ss. cloth.

A Practical Treatise on Brewing; with Formulas for Public Brewers, and Instructions for Private Families. By W. Black. Fifth Edition. 8vo. 10s. 6 20 NEW WORKS Published By LONGMANS And CO.

Chess Openings. By F. W. Longman, Balliol College, Oxford. Fcp. 8vo. 2s. Gd.

The Law of Nations Considered as Independent Political Communities. By Sir Travers Twiss, D.C.L. 2 vols. 8vo. 80s. or separately, Part I *Peace,* 12s. Part II. *War,* 18s.

Hints to Mothers on the Management of their Health during the Period of Pregnancy and in the Lying-in Room. By Thomas Bull, M.D. Fcp. 5s.

The Maternal Management of Children in Health and Disease. By Thomas Bull, M.D. Fcp. 5».

How to Nurse Sick Children; containing Directions which may be found of service to all who have charge of the Young. By Charles West, M.D. Second Edition. Fcp. 8vo. Is. Gd. Notes on Hospitals. By Florence Nightingale. Third Edition, enlarged; with 13 Plans. Post 4to. 18s.

Notes on Lying-in Institutions; with a Proposal for Organising an Institution for Training Midwives and Midwifery Nurses. By Florence Nightingale. With 5 Plans. Square crown 8vo. 7s. Gd.

The Cabinet Lawyer; a Popular Digest of the Laws of England, Civil, Criminal, and Constitutional. Twenty-third Edition, corrected and brought up to the Present Date. Fcp. 8vo. price 7s. Gd. Willich'S Popular Tables for Ascertaining the Value of Lifehold, Leasehold, and Church Property, Renewal Fines, &c.; the Public Funds; Annual Average Price and Interest on Consols from 1731 to 1867; Chemical, Geographical, Astronomical, Trigonometrical Tables, &c. Post 8vo. 10s.

Pewtner's Comprehensive Specifier; a Guide to the Practical Specification of every kind of Building-Artificer's Work: with Forms of Building Conditions and Agreements, an Appendix, Foot-Notes, and

'Index. Edited by W. Young. Architect. Crown 8vo. Gs. *Periodical Publications.*

The Edinburgh Review, or Critical Journal, published Quarterly in January, April, July, and October. 8vo. price 6s. each Number.

Notes On Books: An Analysis of the Works published during each Quarter by Messrs. Longmans & Co. The object is to enable Bookbuyers to obtain such information regarding the various works as is usually afforded by tables of contents and explanatory prefaces. 4to. Quarterly. *Gratis.*

Fraser's Magazine. Edited by James ANTnoxv Froude, M.A. New Series, published on the 1st of each Month. 8vo. price 2s. Gd. each Number.

The Alpine Journal; A Record of Mountain Adventure and Scientific Observation. By Members of the Alpine Club. Edited by Leslie Stephen. Pub-

lished Quarterly. May 31, Aug. 31, Nov. 30, Feb. 28. 8vo. price Is. *Gd.* each Number.
*Knowledge* for The Stepping Stone to Knowledge:
Containing upwards of Seven Hundred Questions and Answers on Miscellaneous
Subjects, adapted to the capacity of Infant
Minds. By a Mother. New Edition, enlarged and improved. 18mo. price Is.

The Stepping Btone to Geography:
Containing several Hundred Questions and
Answers on Geographical Subjects. 18-mo. Is.

The Stepping Stone t o English History:
Containing several Hundred Questions and
Answers on the History of England. Is.

The Stepping Stone to Bible Knowledge: Containing several Hundred Questions and Answers on the Old and New
Testaments. 18mo. Is.

The Stepping Stone to Biography:
Containing several Hundred Questions and
Answers on the Lives of Eminent Men and
Women. 18mo. Is.
the *Young.*

Second Series of the Stepping
Stone to Knowledge: containing upwards of Eight Hundred Questions and Answers on Miscellaneous Subjects not contained in the First Series. 18mo. Is.

The Stepping Stone to French Pronunciation and Conversation: Containing several Hundred Questions and Answers. By Mr. P. Sadler. 18mo. Is.

The Stepping Stone to English Grammar: Containing several Hundred Questions and Answers on English Grammar. By Mr. P. Sadler. 18mo. Is.

The Stepping Stone to Natural History: Vertebrate or Backboned Animals. Part I. *Mammalia*; Part II. *Birds, Reptiles, Fishes.* 18mo. Is. each Part.
INDEX.
Acton's Modern Cookery 19
Allies on Formation of Christendom 15

Allen's Discourses of Chrysostom 16
Alpine Guide (The) 17
Journal 20
Amos's Jurisprudence 5
Anderson's Strength of Materials 9
Abnold's Manual of English Literature.. 6
Authority and Conscience 14
Autumn Holidays of a Country Parson.... 7
Aybe's Treasury of Bible Knowledge 15
Bacon's Essays by Whately 6
Life and Letters, by Spedding.. 4
-Works 5
Bain's Mental and Moral Science 8
on the Senses and Intellect 8
Ball's Guide to the Central Alps 17
Guide to the "Western Alps 17
Guide to the Eastern Alps 17
Bayldon's Rents and Tillages 14
Beaten Tracks 17
Becker's *Charicles* and *Gallus* 18
Benfey's Sanskrit-English Dictionary.... 6
Bernard on British Neutrality 1
Black's Treatise on Brewing 19
Blackley's German-English Dictionary.. 6
Blaine's Rural Sports 19
Veterinary Art 19
Blokam's Metals 9
Booth's Saint-Simon 3
Boultbee on 39 Articles 14
Bourne on Screw Propeller 13
's Catechism of the Steam Engine.. 13
Examples of Modern Engines.. 13
Handbook of Steam Engine.... 13
Treatise on the Steam Engine 13
Improvements in the same 13
Bowdleb's Family Shakspeare 18
Beaddon's Lire in India 16
Bramley-Moore's Six Sisters of the Valley 18
Beande's Dictionary of Science, Literature,
and Art 10
Beay's Manual of Anthropology 7
Philosophy of Necessity 7
On Force 7
(Mrs.) Hartland Forest 17
Beee's Fallacies'of Darwinism 10
Browne's Exposition of the 39 Articles.... 15
Brunel's Life of Brunel 4

Buckle's History of Civilisation 2
Posthumous Remains 7
Bull's Hints to Mothers 20
Maternal Management of Children.. 20
Bunsen's God in History 3
Prayers 14
Burgomaster's Family (The).. 17
Burke's Vicissitudes of Families 5
Burton's Christian Church 3
Cabinet Lawyer 20
Campbell's Norway 18
Cates's Biographical Dictionary 4
and Woodward's Encyclopaedia 8
Cats and Farlie's Moral Emblems 12
Changed Aspects of Unchanged Truths.... 7
Chesney's Indian Polity £
Waterloo Campaign-
Chorale Book for England 12
Christ the Consoler 14
Clougd's Lives from Plutarch 2
Colenso on Pentateuch and Book of Joshua 15
Collins's Perspective 13
Commonplace Philosopher in Town and
Country, by A. K. H. B 7
Conington's Translation of Virgil's jBneid IS
Miscellaneous Writings.... 7
Contanseau's Two French Dictionaries.. 0
Conybeaee and Howson's Life and Epistles
of St. Paul 14
Cooke's Grotesque Animals 12
Coopeb's Surgical Dictionary 11
Copland's Dictionary of Practical Medicine 12
Cotton's Memoir and Correspondence.... 4
Counsel and Comfort from a Cily Pulpit.. 7
Cox's (G.W.) Aryan Mythology 3
Tale of the Great Persian War 2
Tales of Ancient Greece — 17
and Jones's Romances 17
Teutonic Tales.. 17
Creasy on British Constitution 2
Cresy's Encycloposdia of Civil Engineering 13
Critical Essays of a Country Parson 7
Crookes on Beet-Root Sugar 14
— 's Chemical Analysis 11
Culley's Handbook of Telegraphy I3

Cusack's Student's History of Ireland 2
D'aubigne's History of the Reformation in
the time of Calvin 2
Davidson's Introduction to New Testament 15
Dead Shot (The), by Marksman 19
De La Rive's Treatise on Electricity 9
De Morgan's Paradoxes 7
Denison's Vice-Regal Life 1
Disraeli's Lord George Bentinck 4
Novels and Tales 17
Dobson on the Ox 19
Dove's Law of Storms 9
Doyle's Fairyland 12
Drew's Reasons for Faith 14
Dyee's City of Rome 3
22
NEW WORKS Purlished Ry LONGMANS And CO.
Eabtlake,s Gothic Revival IS
Hints on Household Taste.... 13
Eaton,s Musical Criticism and Biography 4
Eden,s Queensland 16
Edinburgh Review 20
Elements of Eotany 10
Ellicott on New Testament Revision. ... 15
,b Commentary on Ephesiaus.... 15
Galatians.... 15
— Pastoral Epist. 15
Philippians,4c. 15
Thessalonians 15
,s Lectures on Life of Christ.... 15
EEichsen,b Surgery 11
Evans,s Ancient Stone Implements 10
Ewald,b History of Israel 15
Fairrairn,b Application of Cast and Wrought Iron to Building 13
——— Information for Engineers.... 13
Treatise on Mills and Millwork 13
Iron Shipbuilding 13
Faraday,b Life and Letters 4
Farrar,s Chapters on Language 6
Families of Speech 7
FitzWYGbaM on Horses and Stables 19
Fowlee,s Collieries and Colliers 19
Francis,s Fishing Book 19
Fraser,s Magazine 20

Freshfield,s Travels in the Caucasus.. .. 16
Froudr,s English in Ireland 1
History of England 1
Short Studies 7
Gamger on Horse-Shoeing 19
Ganot,b Elementary Physics 9
Natural Philosophy 9
Garrod,b Materia Medica 12
Giant (The) 17
Gilreet,s Cadore 16
and Churchill,b Dolomites.... 16
Girdlestone,s Bible Synonyms 14
Girtin,b House I Live In 11
Gledbtone,s Life of Whitefield 4
(soddard,b Wonderful Stories 17
Goldsmith,s Poems, Illustrated 18
Goodeve,s Mechanism 9
Graham,s Autobiography of Milton 4
— View of Literature and Art.... 2
Grant,s Ethics of Aristotle 5
Home Politics 2
Graver Thoughts of a Country Parson 7
Gray,sAnatomy 11
Gripein,s Algebra and Trigonometry. ... 9
Griffith,b Fundamentals 14
Geotr on Correlation of Physical Forces.. 9
Gueney,s Chapters of French History.... 2
Gwilt,b Encyclopasdia of Architecture.... 13
Hartwig,s Harmonies of Nature 10
Polar World 10
i Sea and its Living Wonders.... 10
i Subterranean World 10
Hatherton,b Memoir and Correspondence 2
Hayward,s Biographical and Critical Essays 4
Herschel,s Outlines of Astronomy 7
Hewitt on the Diseases of Women 11
Hodgson,s Time and Space 7
Theory of Practice 7
Holland,s Recollections 4
Holmes,s Surgical Treatment of Children.. 11 System of Surgery 11
Hoene,b Introduction to the Scriptures.. 15
How we Spent the Summer 16
Howitt,s Australian Discovery 17
Rural Life of England 17
Visits to Remarkable Places.... 17

Hurnee,s Pope Sixtus the Fifth 4
Humroldt,s Life 4
Hume,s Essays 8
Treatise on Human Nature 8
Ihne,b History of Rome S
Ingelow,s Poems 18
Story of Doom 18
Jamis,s Christian Counsels 14
J aMebON,s Legends of Saints and Martyrs.. 12
——— Legends of the Madonna 12
Legends of the Monastic Orders 12
Legends of the Saviour 12
Jamieson on Causality 5
Jardine,s Christiau Sacerdotalism 1
Johnbton,s Geographical Dictionary 8
Jones,s Royal Institution 4
KaLiach,a Commentary on the Bible 6
Hebrew Grammar 6
Keith on Destiny of the World 15
Fulfilment of Prophecy 15
Keel,s Metallurgy, by Crookes and R6HBIG 14
Kirry and Spence,b Entomology 9
Lang,s Ballads and Lyrics 18
Lanman,s Japanese in America 16
Latham,s English Dictionary 6
Laughton,s Nautical Surveying' 9
Laveeack,s Setters 19
Lecky,b History of European Morals 3
Rationalism 3
Leaders of Public Opinion 4
Leisure Hours in Town, by A. K. H. B 7
Lessons of Middle Age, by A. K. H. B 7
Lewes,b Biographical History of Philosophy 3
Liddell & Scott,s Greek-English Lexicons 6
Life of Man Symbolised 12
Lindley and Moore,s Treasury of Botany 19
Longman,s Edward the Third 2
Lectures on History of England 2
Chess Openings 20
Loudon,b Encyclopaedia of Agriculture.... 11
Gardening 14
Plants 10
Lurrock,s Origin of Civilisation 10
Lytton,s Odes of Horace 18

Lyra Germanica 12,16
Macaulay,s (Lord) Essays 3
History of England.. 1
Lays of Ancient Rome 18
Miscellaneous Writings 7
  Macaulay's (Lord) Speeches 6
  — Works 1
  MacLEOD'sTrinciples of Political Philosophy 5
  Dictionary of Political Economy 5
  — Theory and Practice of Banking 19
  Mcculloch's Dictionary of Commerce. .. 19
  Maguibe's Life of Father Mathew 4
Pitts IX 15
Mankind, their Origin and Destiny 10
Manning's England and Christendom.... 15
  Maecet's Natural Philosophy 9
  Marshall's Physiology 12
  Mabshman's History of India 2
  Life of Havelock 6
  Mabtineau's Endeavours after the Christian Life 16
  Massingbeed's History of the Reformation 3
  Mathews on Colonial Question 2
  Maundeb's Biographical Treasury 6
  Geographical Treasury 9
  Historical Treasury 8
  Scientific and Literary Treasury 10
  'Treasury of Knowledge 19
  Treasury of Natural History.. 10
  Maxwell's Theory of Heat 9
  May's Constitutional History of England.. 1
  Melville's Digby Grand 18
  General Bounce 18
  Gladiators 18
  'Good for Nothing 18
  'Holmby House 18
  Interpreter 18 Kate Coventry 18
  'Queen's Maries 18
  Mendelssohn's Letters 4
  Meeitale's Pall of the Roman Republic.. 3 . Romans under the Empire 8
  Meeripield's Arithmetic and Mensuration 8
  'Magnetism and Evers's Navigation.. 8
  Meteyabd's Group of Englishmen 4
  Miles on Horse's Foot and Horse Shoeing. 19 on Horses' Teeth and Stables 19

Mill (J.) on the Mind 6
Mill (J. S.) on Liberty 6
Subjection of Women 6 on Representative Government 6 on Utilitarianism 6
's Dissertations and Discussions 6
Political Economy 6
System of Logic 6
Hamilton's Philosophy 6
Milleb's Elements of Chemistry 11
Inorgauio Chemistry 9
Mitchell's Manual of Architecture 13
Manual of Assaying 14
Monsell's Beatitudes 16
His Presence not his Memory.. 16
'Spiritual Songs' 16
Mooee's Irish Melodies 18
Lalla Rookh 18
Poetical Works 18
Mobell's Elements of Psychology 6
Mental Philosophy 6
Mobsman's Christian Church 3
Mulleb's (Mai) Chips from a German Workshop 1
Lectures on the Science of Language B (K. 0.) Literature of Ancient Greece 2
Mr/RChison on Liver Complaints 12
Mube's Language and Literature of Greece 2
Nash's Compendium of the Prayer-Book.. 14 New Testament Illustrated with 'Wood Engravings from the Old Masters 12
Newman's Historyof his Religious Opinion; 6
Nightingale on Hospitals 20
Lying-In Institutions.. 20
Nilsson's Scandinavia 10
Noethcott on Lathes and Turning IS
Notes on Books 20
Odling's Course of Practical Chemistry.. 11
Outlines of Chemistry 11
Owen's Comparative Anatomy and Physiology of Vertebrate AnimalB 9
Lectures on the Invertebrata 9
Packe's Guide to the Pyrenees 17
Paget's Lectures on Surgical Pathology.. 10
Pebeiea's Elements of Materia Medica.... 12
Pereing's Churches and Creeds 14
Pewtneb's Comprehensive Specifier 20
Pictures in Tyrol 16

Piesse's Art of Perfumery 14
Playeb-feowd's California 16
Peendebgast's Mastery of Languages — 6
Peescoit's Scripture Difficulties 15
Present-Day Thoughts, by A. K H. B 7
Peoctoe's Astromomical Essays 8
'Orbs around Us 8
Plurality of Worlds 8
Saturn 8
Scientific Essays 9
Star Atlas 8
Star Depths 8
Sun 8
Public Schools.Atlas 8
Rae's Westward by Rail 16
Ranken on Strains in Trusses 13
Rawlin Son's Parthia 2
Recreations of a Country Parson, by A. K. H. B 7
Reeve's Royal and Republican France.... 2
Reichel's See of Rome 11
Reilly's Map of Mont Blanc 17
Rivebs's Rose Amateur's Guide 10
Rogees's Eclipse of Faith 7
Defence of Faith 7
Roget's Thesaurus of English Words and Phrases 6
Ronalds's Fly-Fisher's Entomology 19
Rose's Loyola
Rothschild's Israelites 15
Russell's Pau and the Pyrenees 16
Bandabs's Justinian's Institutes 6
Sanfoed's English Kings 1
Savile on Truth of the Bible IS
Schellen's Spectrum Analysis 8
Scott's Lectures on the Fine Arts 12
Albert Durer 12
Seaside Musing, by A. K. H. B 7
Bbebohm's Oxford Reformers of 1498 2 24 NEW WORKS Published By LONGMANS And CO.
Sewell's After Life 17
Glimpse of the World 17
History of the Early Church.... 3
Journal of a Home Life 16
Passing Thoughts on Religion.. 16
Preparation for Communion.... 16
Readings for Confirmation 16
Readings for Lent 16
Examination for Confirmation.. 16

Stories and Talcs 17
'Thoughts for the Age 16
Thoughts for the Holy Week.... 16
Shipley's Essays on Ecclesiastical Reform 14
Short's Church History 8
Smi Id's Paul's Voyage and Shipwreck.... 11 (sydney) Lire and Letters 4
Miscellaneous Works.. 7
Wit and Wisdom 7 (Dr. R. A.) Air and Rain 8
Southey's Doctor 6
Poetical Works 18
Stanley': History of British Birds 9
Stephen's Ecclesiastical Biography 4
Playground of Europe 16
Stcpping-Stone to Knowledge, &c 20
Stiemng's Protoplasm 7
Secret of Hegel 7
Sir William Hamilton 7
Stockmab's Memoirs 1
Stonehenge on the Dog 19 on the Greyhound 19
Steicexand's Queens of England 4
Sunday Afternoons at the Parish Church of a University City, by A. K. H. B 7
Taylob's History of India 2 (Jeremy) Works, edited by Eden 16
Text-Books of Science 8
Text-booes or Science 9
Thielwaxl's History of Greece 2
Thomson's Laws of Thought 5

New World of Being 7
Thudichum's Chemical Physiology 11
Todd (A.) on Parliamentary Government.. 1 and Bowman's Anatomy and Physiology of Man 12
Tbench's Realities of Irish Life 2
Teoixope's Barchester Towers 18
Warden IS
Twiss's Law of Nations 20
Tyndall's Diamagnetism 9
Faraday as a Discoverer 4
Fragments of Science 9
Hours of Exercise in the Alps.. 16
Tyndall's Lectures on Electricity 9
Lectures on Light 9
Lectures on Sound 9
Heat a Mode of Motion 9
Molecular Physics 11
Uebeeweg's System of Logic 7
Tjee's Dictionary of Arts, Manufactures, and Mines 13
Van Dee Hceven's Handbook of Zoology.. 10
Vogan's Doctrine of the Euchrist 14
Watson's Geometry 9
Principles and Practice of Physic 11
Watts's Dictionary of Chemistry 11
Webb's Objects for Common Telescopes.... 8
Webstee & Wilkinson's Greek Testament 15

Wellington's Life, by Gleig 4
West on Children's Diseases 11 on Children's Nervous Disorders.... 11 on Nursing Sick Children 26
Whately's English Syuonyines 6
Logic 5
Rhetoric 6
White and Riddle's Latin Dictionaries.. 6
Wilcocks's Sea Fisherman 19
Williams's Aristotle's Ethics 6
Willi Ams on Consumption 11
Willich's Popular Tables 20
Willis's Principles of Mechanism 13
Winslow on Light 9
Wood's (J. G.) Bible Animals 10
Homes without Hands.... 9 . Insects at Home 10
Insects Abroad 10
Strange Dwellings 9 (T.) Chemical Notes 11
Wobdswoeth's Christian Ministry 14
Yarndale 17
Tonge's History of England 1
English-Greek Lexicons 6
Horace 18
English Literature 5
Modern History 3
Youatt on the Dog 19 on the Horse 19
Zelleb's Socrates 3
—— Stoics, Epicureans, and Sceptics.. 3
Zigzagging amongst Dolomites 15

Lightning Source UK Ltd.
Milton Keynes UK
UKOW02f2006230314

228663UK00005B/49/P